♣ EASY ♠
CARD TRICKS

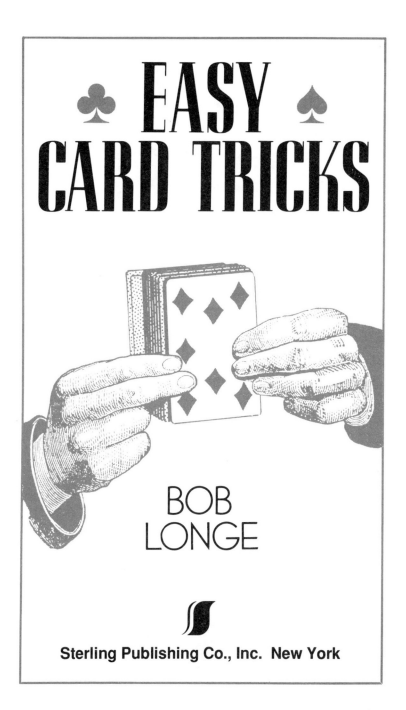

♣ EASY ♠
CARD TRICKS

BOB
LONGE

Sterling Publishing Co., Inc. New York

Library of Congress Cataloging-in-Publication Data

Longe, Bob, 1928–
    Easy card tricks / by Bob Longe.
        p.   cm.
    Includes index.
    ISBN 0-8069-0950-1
    1. Card tricks.   I. Title.
    GV1549.L526   1995
    795.4'38—dc20   94-25142
                                CIP

10   9   8   7   6   5

Published by Sterling Publishing Company, Inc.
387 Park Avenue South, New York, N.Y. 10016
© 1995 by Bob Longe
Distributed in Canada by Sterling Publishing
% Canadian Manda Group, One Atlantic Avenue, Suite 105
Toronto, Ontario, Canada M6K 3E7
Distributed in Great Britain and Europe by Cassell PLC
Wellington House, 125 Strand, London WC2R 0BB, England
Distributed in Australia by Capricorn Link (Australia) Pty Ltd.
P.O. Box 6651, Baulkham Hills, Business Centre, NSW 2153, Australia
Manufactured in the United States of America
All rights reserved

Sterling ISBN 0-8069-0950-1

Contents

INTRODUCTION

Some of the finest card tricks in the world appear in this book. Not one of them requires any sleight of hand, but these tricks are still of professional calibre. Many of them have fooled and amazed other magicians. I'll be amazed if you don't find at least a dozen which you like and will perform regularly.

The tricks presented here are by no means automatic. Consider each trick as a basic "recipe." Add to it practice, patter, and a big dollop of *you*. *Your* personality makes the trick. I've included suggestions for patter, but say things *your* way, sprinkle in your own wry remarks, make up your own story.

As with any recipe, change the trick to suit your taste; eliminate and add until you have something that suits your "palate." You'll have a trick that is truly yours and which will be "appetizing" to others.

DEVELOPING A ROUTINE

Several excellent routines can be built around the tricks in this book. How many tricks to use in a routine? There's no right answer. You should be ready to perform as many as seven or eight tricks, but when interest wanes, immediately go to your climactic blockbuster.

You might finish eight tricks, and your audience clamors for more. Usually, I'll perform a few more tricks. The important thing is to quit on a high note. Don't wait until your audience drifts. Don't let yourself get carried away with your performance. Some magicians, when the audience grows apathetic, will say something like, "Here! Let me show you this one." You want to be admired, not pitied. It's better to stop a trick or two short than to show even one trick too many.

It's also true that some groups will want to see every trick you can show them. In this case, I'd recommend that you do your first routine, and follow it with a shorter routine which also has a strong closing trick. Then quit. Save a little something for next time.

How to develop a routine? For the most part, it's a matter of trial and error, but there are a few fundamentals. The first trick should be an attention-getter, and it shouldn't be lengthy. The last trick should be one of your best, leaving a strong favorable impression. In between, you should have considerable variety.

You have at least three possible themes for your routine:

(1) Do an entire "mental" routine, choosing several tricks from the section, *All in the Mind* (pages 75–91). Sufficient variety is provided as you read minds, predict the future, and perform other psychic feats. You are *not* doing card tricks; you are demonstrating peculiar phenomena.

(2) Choose tricks which are strong on audience participation. Eleven of the tricks in the book *require* the assistance of at least two spectators. Of these, six call for three or more spectators. "The more the merrier" definitely applies here.

(3) Perform a number of different types of card trick. I choose some tricks with strong audience participation, and I might pick out a mental trick or two. Emphasize diversity.

An excellent opening trick would be *Easy Opener* (p. 62). The trick is arresting and it has strong spectator involvement. Another good opener would be *Count Off* (p. 14). You might choose an opener in which some of the cards are prearranged. *Cutting the Aces* (p. 70) is a quick, startling miracle, and *Most Magicians* (p. 68) is a snappy routine in itself.

Eventually, you'll find an opening trick which you really like and which works well for you.

To fill out your routine, choose a trick or two from each of the various chapters.

HIDE & SEEK. In this section, you'll find a number of "discovery" tricks. I particularly enjoy performing *Poker Location* (page 18) and *Computer Whiz* (p. 23), but you should try them all.

MAGIC SPELLS. A spelling trick always goes over well, and here you find four of them. My favorite is *Number, Please* (page 42).

UNEXPECTED REVERSALS. Audiences love a trick in which a chosen card mysteriously turns face up. Particularly clever is *Fan Out* (page 48).

RED-&-BLACK MAGIC. These tricks involve red and black cards. All three are clever and effective.

LONG-DISTANCE CALLS. Here are three captivating tricks in which the telephone is used. *Something to Sniff At* (page 60) is a real gem.

SPECIAL ARRANGEMENTS. All six of these tricks depend on the use of prearranged cards. Because of this, you should probably save them for opening tricks, or for occasions on which you're going to perform only one trick. Nothing looks more suspicious than taking out a different deck to perform a particular trick.

There is, however, a clever way in which you can switch decks. Assume you've just finished your routine with a superb trick. Put the cards in the card case and put the case in your pocket. Suppose onlookers insist that you do more. Reach into that same pocket and remove a duplicate deck in which some of the cards have been set up. Perform one of the tricks from this section, followed by a few impromptu tricks.

ALL IN THE MIND. Here you have "mental" tricks. As part of your routine, you might choose a few of these. I find *You Might Wonder* (page 75) particularly arresting.

ASSORTED DANDIES. Any one of these excellent tricks would be a strong closing trick, but I'm particularly fond of *Weight for Me* (page 92), *The Counter* (page 108), *The Queen's Quilt* (page 111), and *Quadruple Coincidence* (page 122).

To begin with, fashion at least one fairly long routine and one short routine to use as a possible follow-up. Practise all these tricks until their performance is second-nature to you. You'll feel confident and *secure,* and your performance will be polished and entertaining.

HIDE & SEEK

Lucky Card Location

The spectator seems to make all the choices, yet you end up finding the chosen card. F. J. Baker had the original trick, which required a blank card. Since I seldom have one, I changed the handling slightly.

You must have a complete 52-card deck. Have Leonard shuffle the deck. Take the cards back, saying, "I have to find my lucky card. If all goes well, it will help with our next experiment." Fan through the cards with faces towards you. You must count to the 25th card. It will help allay spectator suspicion if you count the cards in groups of three. (Separate the cards after you count off 25.) The 26th card from the bottom is on the face of the pile in your left hand (Illus. 1).

Illus. 1

"Here's my lucky card," you declare. Name the card. "If it's to do any good, we'll have to turn it over." Turn it over in place. Close up the cards. Turn the deck face down. The

26th card from the bottom is now face up in the face-down deck.

Hand the deck back to Leonard, saying, "Please think of a number from one to ten." Turn away. "Count off that number of cards from the top and place them in your pocket or hide them somewhere else. I don't want to know your number." Pause. "Now look at the card that lies at that same number from the top and show it around. But make sure to keep it at that same number. For instance, if your number was three, you would look at the third card from the top. Be sure to remember that card because now that's your lucky card."

Turn back to the group. "We have my lucky card turned face up somewhere in the deck. Now let's try my lucky number. I wanted a lucky number that no one else had, so I chose 13. Please deal off 13 cards into a pile." Leonard does so. "Now into another pile, deal as many cards as you want, but make sure you deal past my lucky card, or this trick won't work."

When Leonard finishes, pick up the second pile he dealt and turn it face up. "Take the other pile, Leonard. Let's deal our cards into separate piles. I'll deal mine face up; you deal yours face down. We'll do it together, so we match each other card for card. When we come to my face-down card, we'll stop." Immediately after dealing off your face-down card, stop the deal. Turn the card over, saying, "There it is . . . my lucky card." Ask him to name the card he chose. Point to the last card he dealt and ask him to turn it over. "Look at that; there's *your* lucky card."

Prints of Magic

Walter Gibson invented the main idea; I've combined it with a wonderful old trick.

You must know the name of the top card. A good way is to sneak a peek at the bottom card and, in an overhand shuffle, bring that bottom card to the top of the deck. Ask Henry to think of any number from 1 to 20, and to deal off that many cards into a pile on the table.

"Now," you tell Henry, "cut the remainder of the deck into two piles." After he does so, ask him to shuffle one of the two piles. Then he is to shuffle the other pile. Finally, point to the pile he first dealt off. "Please pick up those cards and hold them facing you so that you can see the bottom card but I can't. Remember that bottom card. Now, if you don't mind, just put your thumbprint on the face of that card, right around the middle."

Pick up one of the other two piles and show Henry exactly how to affix his thumbprint (Illus. 2). Say, "I'll turn away while you put your thumbprint on the face of your card." Turn away for a moment and give these instructions: "Now shuffle that pile. Then put it together with the other piles and give the entire deck a shuffle." The card he "chose" is, of course, the card you originally peeked at.

Illus. 2

Turn back and take the pack from Henry. Turn the top card face up and ask Henry to put his right thumbprint on the face of that card. (If it happens that the top card is the one he chose, take a bow, and *quit!*) Stare at the card, ostensibly studying the thumbprint. "Very interesting. Should be easy to identify."

Set the card face up on the table. Turn the deck face up and begin spreading the cards out, glancing back and forth from the deck to the thumb-printed card as you try to find a match. Act this out, pausing here and there to study a possibility. It works well to *go past* the chosen card and, after spreading out several more, go back to it. Pick it up and compare it closely with the other card. "An exact match!" you declare. "This must be your card."

Count Off

I came across this trick in a magic magazine, where it was referred to as an "old trick." I performed it for several months, and then I realized that I had invented the trick decades earlier. Over the years, however, someone had added a refinement which enhances the effect. Here's the new, improved version.

Have Lillian thoroughly shuffle the deck. Spread the cards out face up, showing how thoroughly the cards are mixed. Note the top and bottom cards. Add them together. Suppose the top card is a five and the bottom is a seven. The sum is 12. Turn the deck face down and start to spread the cards out, offering the choice of a card. As you do so, secretly count off 12 cards and hold these slightly separate from the rest (Illus. 3). (The number you count off is the same as

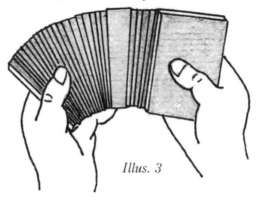

Illus. 3

the total of the top and bottom cards. When you count off the cards, count in groups of three.) Make sure the card is chosen from below these. After Lillian looks at the card and shows it around, lift off the top 12 cards and extend the rest of the deck for her to replace the card. Place the 12 cards on top, even up the deck, and set the deck on the table. From this point on, don't touch the cards.

It's time for a bit of distraction. Address the spectators: "The deck was thoroughly shuffled by Lillian, who then freely selected a card. I haven't changed the position of a single card in the deck. Yet, if we're lucky, we'll see a miracle." Gesture towards the deck. "Lillian, please cut off a *large* chunk of cards." You want to make sure she cuts off well over half the deck. "Notice . . . complete freedom of choice." Point to the small packet, the former lower portion of the deck. "Please turn this pile face up." Call attention to the value of the bottom card of the pile. "Now pick up the other packet and deal into a pile that same number of cards."

Now have her turn the dealt pile face up. She notes the value of the bottom card and deals that many into a third pile. This pile is also turned up, the bottom card noted, and that many dealt into yet another pile.

"Enough piles, right? So what was the name of the chosen card?" After it's named, have Lillian turn the last pile face up. There's the chosen card.

I am always a little surprised at the conclusion. *Three* different cards are counted off from a *shuffled* deck, and the chosen card is found.

Note

At the beginning, when you fan through to add the top and bottom cards, the total may be unusually high—20, for instance. When this occurs, have the cards reshuffled.

The Fooler

I call this trick *The Fooler* because magician Wally Wilson completely fooled me with this one. The secret is extremely subtle.

Ask Kevin to shuffle the deck thoroughly. "Now please think of a number from 5 to 15 and deal that many cards into a face-up pile." Start to turn away, *but* before your back is turned, catch a glimpse of the first card Kevin deals. That first card is your key card. That's it! You're all done with the sneaky portion of the trick.

"Look at the last card you dealt. That's your chosen card. In other words, your card is the one that's at your chosen number. Now cut off a pile from the top of the deck and set it on the table. Pick up the cards you dealt off, turn them face down, and place them on top of the pile in your hands. Put the pile you cut off on top of all."

Turn back to the audience. "There's no doubt now that your chosen card is buried in the middle of the deck where I can't possibly find it." Have Kevin give the deck a few complete cuts.

Take the deck and fan the cards face up before you, staring at one and then another. No luck. Shake your head. "I can't seem to get a picture of your card. Maybe this will help . . . What was the number you thought of?" Suppose Kevin tells you 13. Still puzzled, you fan back and forth through the face-up cards. When you spot your key card, start with that card and count 13 cards towards the face of the deck. The 13th one is the selected card.

Tentatively remove the card and place it face down on the table. "Maybe this is it. What was your card?" Success!

The Divining One

To perform this, you'll need the assistance of five spectators. Ask one spectator to shuffle the deck and then deal it into five equal piles. He will, of course, have two cards left over. These are set aside.

Pick up one of the two cards, saying, "This will have to be my divining card. If all goes well, it will help me find the selected cards." Sneak a look at the face of the card as you touch it to the top of each of the piles (Illus. 4). This is your key card. Then, as you continue speaking, casually set the card a few inches on the far side of the other card. "I'd like five different people to each look at the top card of one of these piles. Remember that card and place it back on top of its pile."

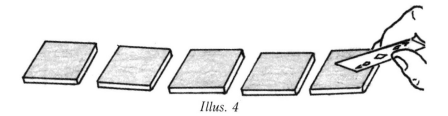

Illus. 4

After they've done so, have a spectator gather up the piles one on top of the other. As he starts, pick up the closest card to you of the two on the table. (The other is the one you secretly peeked at.) "I'll need the divining card," you say, "but you might as well set the other card in there." Chances are that he'll place that other card on the top or bottom of one of the piles as he gathers the cards up. If he seems about to push it *into* a pile, however, you must instantly say, "Just put it on top of any of the piles."

Once the cards are gathered, each of the participants gives the deck a complete cut. Spread the deck face up on the table. Pass the "divining card" over the spread several times. "I think I'm getting the right vibrations," you say. Set the card down. Close up the deck, pick it up, and fan it, faces towards you. Find your key card. Cut the deck so that it becomes the bottom card—that is, the card on the face of the deck. Remove the top card of the deck, touch it to the "divining card," and say, "Yes, that's one." Place the card face down on the table.

Every tenth card after your key card is one of those selected. So, with the cards facing you, fan through from the bottom, casually counting to the tenth card *after* the key card. When you remove this one card, separate the pile you've fanned off so that you'll know where to start the next count. As you locate each card, touch it to the divining card, mumble your approval, and place the card face down on the table.

Finally, turn one of the cards on the table face up. Suppose it is the queen of hearts. "Who had the queen of hearts?" Hand it to the spectator who replies. Repeat with the other four cards.

Poker Location

Milt Kort called my attention to this old trick. This version is by Hen Fetsch; I made some minor simplifications.

The trick is performed while you and the spectators are seated at a table.

Ask a spectator to shuffle the deck and place it on the table. Say to the spectator, "Please cut off half the deck and place it on the table." Point to the former lower section of the deck, and ask the spectator on your left to take the top card of this section. Working clockwise, you have three more spectators each remove a card from the top of this pile. Finally, *you* take one from the top of the pile. "Everyone please look at your card and remember it." You do likewise.

Place your card back on top of the pile. Going *counter-clockwise,* the spectators replace their cards on top. Have someone put either pile on top of the other. Each participant gives the pack a complete cut.

Take the pack. Fan though, faces towards yourself, saying, "I need to find my lucky poker card. In a game of five-card stud, I once filled a straight flush with this . . . Ah, there it is—my lucky poker card!" Name the card.

Actually, you fan through to the card you took from the deck. Count this card as "one" and continue counting as you push the cards into your right hand one by one. When you reach card number 15, stop. Cut the cards so that card number 15 becomes the top card of the deck. Call attention to the bottom (face) card of the deck, calling it, as above, your lucky poker card. Toss the card face up onto the middle of the table.

The chosen cards should now be 11th, 12th, 13th, 14th, and 15th from the top. Deal out five poker hands in the regular way, the last hand going to yourself. Ask the spectators not to look at their cards. Make sure the cards are kept in a pile in the order in which they're dealt.

Each spectator picks up his hand, holding it face down. Then demonstrate with your cards as you give these instructions: "Don't peek at your cards. Now please move your top card to the bottom. Turn the next card face up and put it on top of my lucky poker card on the table. The next card goes to the bottom, and the next one goes face up on top of my lucky poker card. Keep going until you have only one card left."

When all are finished, declare the name of your chosen card and turn it over. Ask the spectator on your left what his card was. Have him turn it over. Do the same for the other three spectators. Each is left with his selected card.

Note

As explained, the trick is performed with four spectators. You may, however, perform it with either more or fewer. In the version above, you find your lucky poker card (the card you originally took from the deck). Counting this card as "one," you count off a total of 15, and cut the cards so that card number 15 becomes the top card of the deck. The number 15 is derived by multiplying the total number of hands by three.

As described above, five hands are dealt, so the number used is 15. Suppose only three spectators are assisting. Only four hands would be dealt. Multiply that by three, and you get 12. So, instead of 15, you use the number 12.

If five spectators are helping, you'll have a total of six hands. Six times three is 18, which is the number you'll use.

It's Nice to See Your Back

This trick was originated by Ben Christopher and expanded on by Roy Walton.

A little preparation is necessary. Suppose you're working with a blue-backed deck. Take a card from a red-backed

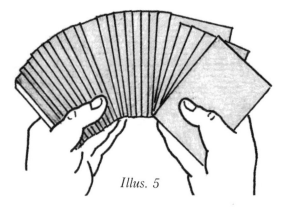

Illus. 5

deck. Remove the duplicate of that card from the blue-backed deck. Now place the red-backed card 15th from the bottom of your deck. You're ready to perform.

Remove the deck from its case and fan out about half the cards face down, saying, "We're going to have two of you merely *think* of cards from this deck" (Illus. 5). Close up the deck. You've subtly put across the point that the backs are all the same.

Ask Spectator 1 to cut off a small packet of cards from the top. Turn the deck face up and have Spectator 2 cut off a small packet from the bottom. (Make sure both spectators cut off fewer than 15 cards.) Ask your two assistants to turn away and secretly count their cards.

"Both of you have counted your cards, so each of you now has a number in mind." Turn to Spectator 1. Ask her to note and remember the card that lies at her number. From the face-up deck, count aloud as you deal 14 cards into a pile on the table, reversing their order. Spectator 1 now has her card. Pick up the pile and replace it on the face of the pack.

Ask Spectator 2 to note and remember the card that lies at her number. Deal and count aloud 14 cards, exactly as before. Pick up the 14-card packet and place it *beneath* the face-up deck.

Still holding the cards face up, say, "We'd better have a complete deck." Hold out your hand to Spectator 1. She gives you her packet of cards, which you place *beneath* the face-up deck. Spectator 2's packet goes on top of the face-up deck.

Spread the pack face up on the table. "Sometimes one card will stand out from the others," you explain. "I hope that's the case." Separate various cards, moving your hand back and forth over the spread. Actually, you're counting down to the 15th card from the top. Eventually, push this one card out of line, saying, "This one really stands out." Address Spectator 1. "Does this happen to be your card?" It does.

Close up the spread and pick up the cards. Turn the pack face down. "Sometimes you can get an even stronger impression by studying the backs of the cards." Spread the pack out face down. One red-backed card stands out among the blue backs. Push this card out of line. Ask Spectator 2, "What was the name of your card?" She names it and you turn it over.

The 10-Card Trick

A favorite of Harry Blackstone, Sr., this trick can involve as many as five spectators. Three, however, seems to work best for me. I've added a few touches.

Assume you're going to get three spectators to assist you. Ask one of them to shuffle the deck and take any ten cards for himself. Have the other spectators do the same. Take the remaining cards and set them aside.

"When I turn away, I'd like each of you to think of a number from one to ten. Then fan through your cards and see which card lies at that number from the top. Please remember your card *and* your number."

When you turn back, you will, in effect, transfer five cards from the top to the bottom of each spectator's pile. What you actually do is transfer *fifteen* cards from the top to the bottom in a phony shuffle.

Take the first spectator's packet, saying, "I'd better mix these a bit." Transfer cards from the top to the bottom of the packet, moving one, two, or three cards each time. As you do so, silently keep track. When you have transferred fifteen, quit. Return the packet to the spectator. Quickly perform the same "shuffle" for the other two spectators and return their packets.

Since the number you move each time is arbitrary, it appears that you're actually mixing the cards. In no time, you will be so used to the procedure that you can actually chat while doing it.

"Do you all remember your number? Good. I'll turn away once more. Then I'd like each of you to transfer that number of cards from the top to the bottom of your pile. For instance, if your number was four, you would move four cards from the top to the bottom *one at a time!*"

This time when you turn back, say, "I'd like each of you to take your top card and place it on the bottom. Then deal the next one onto the table. Then the next one goes on the bottom; the next on the table. Continue until you have just one card left. But please don't peek at that last card. Just hang on to it."

Finally, each spectator is holding one card face down. Ask the first spectator to name his selected card and then to turn over the one he's holding. Have the other two spectators do the same. Naturally, each is holding his chosen card.

Computer Whiz

Robert Neale invented the basic trick, using only the kings and queens. I added eight more cards, along with a few new notions, and ended up with a routine featuring three big surprises. It's an interesting, unusual, colorful trick. Dan Harlan suggested that I add a new ending to the trick, and mentalist Marv Long offered a patter suggestion which brought everything together.

"I'd like to tell you about my new computer dating service," you announce as you begin fanning through the deck, faces towards yourself. Remove the face cards and the tens from the deck, tossing them face up onto the table. "I'm taking all the ladies and gentlemen from the deck. The kings and jacks are men, of course. And the queens are women. But, of course, the tens are also women.

By this time you should have the kings, queens, jacks and tens lying face up on the table. Set the rest of the deck aside. Gather up the group on the table and fan them out, faces towards yourself. Now place two face-down piles onto the table. (At the end, I'll explain how I do this and how the setup can be easily memorized.) In one pile, these should be the face-down cards, *from the bottom up* (the KS being the bottom card):

KS QS JC 10C 10D JD QH KH

In the other pile, these are the face-down cards, *from the bottom up:*

KC QC JS 10S 10H JH QD KD

As you perform the setup, explain, "We're going to computerize the names of these ladies and gentlemen, so that they can be retrieved whenever we wish. In other words, we're installing them on the hard drive." When the two piles are arranged on the table, ask Edith to help out.

Turn away and say to her, "Now we want to have our first customer of the computer dating service. So, please pick up one of the piles, Edith, and fan it out so that you can see all the cards. Then just *think* of one of the cards. It can be either a man or a woman; it can be a red or a black card. In other words, it can be a person with either red hair or black hair. When you have your card, close up the fan and put that pile on top of the other one."

Turn back and pick up the packet on the table. "Now we must program the computer. As you know, computers work on a binary system, so all our programming will be based on the number two. For instance, you had a choice of *two* piles."

Hold the packet from above in your left hand. With the thumb and fingers of your right hand, draw off the top and

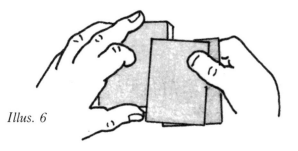

Illus. 6

bottom cards together (Illus. 6). This is known as *milking* the deck. Place the two cards face down to the left. Again draw off the top and bottom cards together. Place them to the right of the first pile of two cards. "Milk" the next two cards from the packet and place them on top of the pile on the left. The next two are "milked" and placed onto the pile on the right. Continue alternating like this until all the cards are placed into two piles.

Pick up one of the piles and fan out the cards with the faces towards Edith. "Is your card here?" you ask. Whatever she answers, the pile containing her card must go *on top* of the other pile. If she says no, close up the cards, pick up the pile on the table and place it on top of the one in your hand. If she says yes, close up the cards and drop them on top of the pile on the table. Pick up the packet.

"We need to feed the computer more information." Holding the packet in the dealing position in your left hand, push off the top two cards and raise them above the others about half of their length. Push off the next two cards and lower them so that they extend below the first two about half their length. Push off the next two and raise them as you did the

Illus. 7

first pair (Illus. 7). The next two are pushed off and lowered as you did with the second pair. Continue through the packet, alternating up and down pairs.

When you finish, with your palm-down right hand grasp the raised group and pull (or strip) them from the others (Illus. 8). Still holding the lower group in your left hand, fan

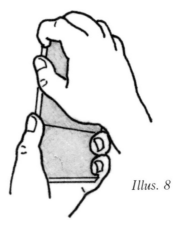

Illus. 8

out the other eight cards so that Edith can see the faces (Illus. 9). If this move is uncomfortable, set the cards which are in your left hand onto the table while you do the fanning.)

Illus. 9

Ask Edith if her card is in the group you're showing her. Whatever she answers, remember that the group in which her card lies must go *beneath* the other group.

Repeat the up-and-down procedure with the cards and, again, strip out the upper group. Show this group to Edith and ask if her card is there. This time, the group in which her card lies goes *on top* of the other group.

At the very beginning of the trick, the group from which Edith selects a card goes on top. After you milk the cards, the group in which her card lies goes on top. With the first up-and-down maneuver, the group in which her card lies goes *beneath* the other group. In the second up-and-down maneuver, the group in which her card lies goes on top. In other words, the only time her pile goes beneath the other pile is when you do the *first* up-and-down maneuver.

"We're almost done programming," you say, "and we're still using the binary system." Fan off the top two cards of the deck and place them onto the table, keeping them in the same order. Fan off the next two and place them to the right of the first two. Fan off the next two and place them on top of the first pair. Fan off the next two and place them on top of the second pair. Continue alternating like this until all sixteen cards have been placed into two piles.

"The computer is ready. I think it'd be wonderful if the computer could provide us with the name of the card you chose to be our first customer. But my program is set up so that it'll only provide information bit by bit—or byte by byte. I'm going to ask you some questions. You can lie or tell the truth—it doesn't matter. The computer has been fed the proper information, and it never misses. Well, hardly ever. First question: What sex is the card you thought of? Was it a man, like a king or jack? Or was it a woman, like a queen or ten?"

Edith answers. Lift off the *top card* of the pile on the right, turn it over and display it, still holding it. Toss it forward face up, as though dealing it. (This is the only time you use the top card of the pile on the right; the rest of the time, you turn the entire pile over.) It'll give the proper sex of the chosen card. (If the card was a king, for example, this card would be a jack.) Comment on Edith's veracity. If she lied, for instance, tell her that she can't possibly fool the computer.

Casually turn over the card you tossed out face up, pick up the remainder of the pile on the right and place it onto the card. This pile should be placed forward and to the left.

Pick up the remaining eight-card pile and deal it into two piles, two cards at a time, just as you did before. "Next question: What color is your card—red or black? In other words, was it a person with black hair or red hair?" After she answers, turn over the pile on the right, showing the bottom card. This will be of the proper color. (If she chose a heart, for example, this would be a diamond.) Make a comment on the unerring accuracy of the computer as you turn the pile face down and set it *to the right* of the first pile you discarded.

Pick up the remaining four-card pile and deal it into two piles as before. "What was the suit of your card?" you ask. After she responds, you provide the correct answer by turning over the pile on the right. Turn this pair face down and place it to the right of the other two discarded piles.

You have two cards remaining. Deal the first to the left and the second to the right. "What was the value of your card?" The card on the right discloses the correct value. Turn this card face down and set it a bit to one side.

"So what was the name of your card?" The remaining card is it. Turn it over and leave it in place.

"So we've found the person you chose, but we haven't found her (him) a date." Suppose the chosen card is the queen of hearts. "So we have this lovely lady. We should line her up with at least four possible dates. Do you think she would prefer men with black hair or men with red hair?"

Here's the situation: On the table you have three piles of cards. The pile on the left, Pile 1, has 8 cards. The pile to the right of it, Pile 2, has 4 cards. And the pile on the far right, Pile 3, has 2 cards. In addition, you have a face-down card which you have set a bit to one side, and you have the face-up chosen card.

Edith chooses. Suppose she elects to have men with red hair. Red is the same color as the selected card. When someone selects the same color as the selected card, you proceed as follows:

Pick up the chosen card, turn it face down, and place it on top of Pile 1. Pick up Pile 1 and place it onto Pile 2. Place the combined piles onto Pile 3. Place all on top of the card you set aside. (The piles will always be gathered up with Pile 1 going onto Pile 2, and the combined pile going onto Pile 3.)

"Let's see if the computer can generate some dates for the young lady." As before, fan off the top two cards of the deck and place them onto the table, keeping them in the same order. In the same way, deal off two cards to the right of these. Two more are dealt onto the pile on the left, and then two more onto the pile on the right. You've now dealt 8 cards, four in each pile. Just as you dealt these cards, deal the remaining 8 cards into two piles that are forward of the first two.

Turn over the top card of each packet. In the example, you'll have two red jacks and two red kings.

When someone selects the color opposite to that of the selected card, proceed as follows:

Place the card you'd set aside on top of Pile 2. Turn the chosen card face down and also place it on top of Pile 2. (Pile 2 now has the chosen card on top; below it is the card you'd set aside; below these two are four more cards.) Gather up the piles and deal them out, as explained—that is, Pile 1 goes onto Pile 2, and the combined pile goes onto Pile 3. Then four piles are formed, as described above. The four top cards are turned over. In this event, the four cards would be two black jacks and two black kings.

You might comment, "Who could ask for more—four handsome men (beautiful ladies) to choose from?"

Now for the finale. Edith has chosen the queen of hearts. Four piles are on the table. Edith had her choice of either red-haired men or black-haired men, so face up on top of the piles are either the black jacks and kings, or the red jacks and kings. Let's say that Edith picked red-haired men.

"Edith, let's suppose you have your choice of these handsome men. Would you pick one of them up, please." She does so. Four piles are on the table; on top of three of these is a face-up card. Turn the face-up cards face down. Here's the placement of the piles as you look at them:

3   4

1   2

Earlier, the spectator chose either red-haired persons or black-haired persons. If the spectator selected persons of the same color as the chosen card, that card is now second from the bottom in Pile 1. If the spectator selected persons with a different hair color, the chosen card is second from the bottom in Pile 3.

"Let's try an experiment. We'll let you do the programming."

Pick up the pile containing the chosen card and hold that pile face down in the left hand. Say to the spectator, "Which pile should go on next?" Whichever she chooses, place it on top of the cards in your left hand. Have her choose another pile and place that one on top. Then place the remaining pile on top.

Say, "You'll have to do some more programming. We'll have to put your potential date into the program. I'm going to form two piles. I'd like you to drop the card you're holding on top of one of the piles whenever you wish. Make sure you drop it face up."

Now you're going to "milk" the cards, as explained earlier. Hold the packet from above in the left hand and draw off the top and bottom cards together with your right hand. Drop these two onto the table. Draw off the top and bottom cards again and place these to the right of the other pile. In the same way, add two to the pile on the left, and then add two to the pile on the right. Continue until the spectator drops his cards on top of one of the piles. At this point, the original chosen card is on the bottom of the pile on the right.

Suppose, however, that the spectator doesn't drop his card onto one of the piles. You'll end up placing a single card on top of the pile on the right. Place the pile on the left on top of the pile on the right. Explain, "Now you're to drop your card face up on top of one of the piles as I deal them." Again milk the cards; this time the original chosen card will be on the bottom of the pile on the left.

At last the spectator places the face-up card on top of one of the piles. Stop dealing immediately.

There are now two possibilities:

(1) If the spectator places the card on top of the pile which has the chosen card on the bottom, have him give that pile a complete cut. Place the cards in your hand onto the table. Say, "Please reassemble the cards. Just place any packet on top of another, and then place those on top of the remaining packet. Do it any way you wish."

(2) If the spectator places the card on top of the pile which *doesn't* have the chosen card on the bottom, have her place *either pile* on top of the other. She then gives the pile a complete cut. If the cut brings the face-up card to the top or bottom, have her cut again. Place the cards in your hand on the table. Say, "Please put one of the piles on top of the other."

The cards are now assembled, and the face-up card is face to face with the original chosen card.

"You're the programmer this time," you say. "You've been making the choices. Complete the programming by giving the cards one more complete cut." Again, if the face-up card comes to the top or bottom, have the spectator cut again.

Let's return to our example. Fan through the cards to the face-up card. Remove it, along with the card above it, and place the pair onto the table. The chosen card is face down on top of the face-up card. "Edith, you originally chose the queen of hearts. And you had four men to choose from. You chose this man." Name the card. "Let's see if this computer dating system really works. Did he also choose you?" Turn the chosen card face up. "Yes! The queen of hearts! I can't believe it. The system actually works. And *you* are a superb programmer."

Note

Here's an easy way to set up the cards. Hold all 16 cards fanned out in your left hand, faces towards you. The first eight you'll choose are:

KS QS JC 10C 10D JD QH KH

Note that the first four go from king down to ten, and the next four go from ten up to king. All you really need to remember is that the first black card is the king of spades and the first red card is the ten of diamonds. The suits run in pairs, and all four suits are represented. First come four blacks and then come four reds.

So you take out the KS and place it face down onto the table. On top of it, place another spade, the QS. You need two more blacks: first the JC, then the 10C. The sequence now reverses, starting with a ten, the 10D. This is followed by the JD. Then come two more reds. Since you must have all four suits, these must be QH and KH.

You're done with Pile 1.

These are the cards in Pile 2:

KC QC JS 10S 10H JH QD KD

This pile is easy. First come the black cards, running from king down to ten. Then come the red cards, running from ten up to king. The KC is the first card placed face down onto the table, and the KD is the card on top of the pile.

It's a Dan-dy

Dan Harlan gave me permission to include this "mathematical" trick. I've included two variations. The principle is similar to that used in the previous trick, but the concept is totally different.

You can perform the trick for several spectators at the same time, but for clarity I'll first explain how you might do it for one person.

Let's assume Frank is assisting you. After he shuffles the pack, have him count off 15 cards. He looks through the 15 cards and thinks of one, after which he shuffles the packet.

Take the packet from him and explain, "I'm going to show you some cards and ask if your card is among them. Whether the answer is yes or no, I'll *always* place that bunch *under* the others. Please remember, I'll always place the cards you look at under the others."

Hold the packet face down. You'll now perform a stripping action similar to that used in *Computer Whiz* (page 23). Alternately push the cards up and down; only instead of pushing two cards each time, you'll only push one. Fan through the cards, pushing the first one up for half its length, the second one down, the third one up, the fourth down, and so on, until you finish the packet.

Then, with your palm-down right hand grasp the upper group and pull (or strip) them from the others (Illus. 8, page 26). Still holding the other group in your left hand, fan out the eight cards so that Frank can see them (Illus. 9, page 27).

"Is your card among these?" you ask. Whatever he answers, you place this eight-card packet below the others. Again go through the up-and-down procedure, strip out the eight upper cards and show them to Frank. Whatever his reply, the eight again go below the others. Repeat this two more times—four times in all. Then announce the exact number of Frank's card from the top. Count down to that number in the packet and show that you're correct.

How do you do it? Simply remember this geometric progression: 1, 2, 4, 8. When you show the cards the first time, if the spectator answers yes, you remember 1, the first number in the progression. On the second showing, if he says yes, add 2 to his total. Each time he answers no, you add *nothing* (that should be easy to remember). On the third showing, add 4 if he says yes. On the fourth showing, add 8 if he says yes. Let's try an example. Show the spectator the cards the first time. He doesn't see his card. Place these cards under the others and remember *zero*. The spectator sees his card in the second group; you remember the number *2*. The third time the spectator also sees his card; you add *4* to the previous *2* and get *6*. Show cards for the fourth time and the spectator doesn't see his card; this means another *zero*. The total, then, is *6*. Announce to the spectator, "I believe that your card is the sixth card down." Count down to the sixth card and show that you're right.

That's the trick in its simplest form. The trick can be made more interesting, more amusing, and *easier* by having two or three spectators participate. (And, in the notes at the end, there's an intriguing version for *one* spectator.) Basically, you make a game of it. Here's how it works.

Frank and Lena agree to help out. "We're going to play a little game to see who can get the most points," you say. But first you have the pack shuffled and 15 cards counted off. While your back is turned, each of the spectators removes one card from the packet and remembers it. The cards are returned, and each of the spectators shuffles the packet.

Turn back to the group, take the packet, and continue, "I'm going to show you some of these cards. If you see your card in that group, you get a point. If you don't, you get nothing. We'll do this several times." In this version, you *don't* mention that each time you will place the packet under the rest of the cards.

Do the up-down maneuver. Show the 8 cards to Frank, asking if his card is there. Show them to Lena, asking if she sees her card. Suppose Frank sees his card and Lena doesn't see hers. "Ah, Frank, you have 1 point. And Lena, you have none. So Frank is ahead 1 to nothing. Let's raise the ante. This time, you get 2 points if you see your card."

Again, do the up-down maneuver. Let's say that both spectators see their card. "So that's 2 points apiece. Frank, you now have 3 points, and Lena has 2. Let's raise it again. This time, we'll make it 4 points."

After the up-down maneuver, Frank doesn't see his card, but Lena sees hers. "You still have 3 points, Frank. And now Lena has 4 more points. She had 1; now she has 5. Finally, we'll give each of you a chance to get 8 points."

Frank sees his card, but Lena doesn't see hers. "Let's see, you had 3 points, Frank. You now have 8 more. This gives you 11 points. I'm sorry, Lena, but you lose. You still have only 5 points." Pause. "Five points. Let's see what card number 5 is." Count aloud as you deal off 5 cards. Ask Lena to name her card. Turn over the last card dealt off; it's hers. Turn Lena's card face down. Return the entire pile of five cards to the top of the packet.

"And, Frank, you had 11 points. Let's see what card 11 is." Count down to that card in the same way, ask the name of his selected card, and show it.

Clearly, you always count to the lower number first.

You can repeat the trick, since it's unlikely that the numbers will recur. You can readily perform with as many as three or four spectators. It's easy to keep track because each spectator will keep a running total of his own score. If you should happen to forget, feel free to ask. It also helps if you keep repeating the score as you go along.

Notes

This trick definitely bears repetition. Do it *at least* twice.

When performing with one spectator, I find it works well to play the same game with *me* as the opponent. Start by proposing that you and the spectator have a contest to see who can get the most points. She shuffles the pack and counts off 15 cards. Take the 15 cards, saying, "First, I'll think of one of these cards." Actually, you fan through and *pretend* to think of one. Give the packet back, have her shuffle and think of one of the cards herself. Again she shuffles the packet.

Take the packet and turn it face up. Fan out several cards from the top of the face-up packet, saying, "Thoroughly mixed." With a quick glance down, note the second card from the top of the face-up packet. (This will be the second card from the bottom when you turn the packet face down.) Look away and casually fan out a few more cards. The card you noted will be the card you "thought of." Close up the packet and turn it face down.

Perform the up-down maneuver. As always, strip out the upper group and show this group to the spectator. "If you see your card, you get a point. If not, I get a point," you explain. Keep a running total of the comparative score as you show the cards four times. As before, the progression is 1, 2, 4, 8.

Suppose that at the completion of the game, the spectator has 9 points. (You'll have 6 in this instance, because the total will always be 15.) Congratulate the spectator on her victory. Then say, "You had 9 points. Let's check the ninth card." Count 8 cards into a pile, one on top of the other, and toss out the ninth card. Ask the name of her card and have her turn over the one you tossed out. As she turns it over, drop the cards in your hand on top of the pile on the table. Take her chosen card, turn it face down, and drop it on top of the stack.

"My number was 6," you say. Count off 6 cards. Name the card you'd peeked at. Turn it over. Sure enough, yours came out also.

Once in a blue moon, the spectator will choose the same card as you do. At the end, when she names her card, simply say, "What a coincidence! That's the same card I thought of." Then repeat the trick.

MAGIC SPELLS

It's Magic

The originator of this trick is (I believe) Patrick Duffie. Milt Kort introduced the trick to me.

Set a thoroughly shuffled deck on the table. Ask Felix and Louise to help out. Say to Felix, "Please cut the deck into three fairly equal piles." When he's done, address Louise: "Choose one of those piles, and put the other two back into the card case."

About one-third of the deck is left on the table. Ask Louise to cut off a small pile from the packet. Felix takes the remaining cards.

Say to Louise, who has the smaller packet, "If I should perform a mysterious feat, would you say, 'It's magic.'?" Whatever she replies, continue, "I'd like you to look at the bottom card of your packet, Louise. That's your chosen card." When she has done so, say, "Now spell out the words 'It's magic,' moving one card from the top to the bottom of your packet for each letter in the spelling."

Guide her through this.

Turn your attention to Felix. "You don't believe in magic, do you, Felix? You think all of this is trickery. In fact, you think that this is a dumb trick. What I'd like you to do is look at the bottom card of your packet and remember it." When he's done so, say, "Now please spell out the sentence 'This is a dumb trick.' Just as Louise did, move one card from the top to the bottom of your packet for each letter in the spelling."

Guide Felix, as well.

"Time for some elimination. I'd like each of you to deal your top card onto the table. Now place your next card underneath the packet. The next card goes on the table, and the next on the bottom of the packet. Keep going until you have only one card left, but please don't look at the card."

Help out as they perform their "down-and-under" deal. At last, each is holding one card face down.

"From the beginning, I haven't touched the cards, right? Nor did I have any way of knowing how many cards each of you would choose. So let's see if I'm magical . . . or not." Ask Louise to name her card. She then turns her last card over; it's the one she chose. Repeat the procedure with Felix.

Notes

The smaller pile must consist of no more than eight cards, and the larger of no more than 16 cards. If you follow the above routine exactly, the numbers should work out.

You can work up patter of your own, if you wish. Any eight-letter sentence will do for the smaller packet, and any 16-letter sentence will work for the larger packet.

In some respects the trick is even more effective when performed for one spectator. After you've eliminated two-thirds of the pack, the spectator cuts off a small pile from the remaining third. Offer the choice of the smaller packet or the larger packet. The pile which isn't chosen is placed in the card case with the other cards. Clearly, you proceed with the spectator looking at the bottom card and then spelling out "It's magic" with the smaller pile, or "This is a dumb trick" with the larger pile. This is followed by the down-and-under deal and the revelation of the chosen card.

Lots of Luck

Magician Wally Wilson showed me a spelling trick that he'd invented. I worked out a way to accomplish a similar effect using a different principle.

Margie's a good sport, so ask her to shuffle the deck. Take it back, saying, "Poker is a game in which luck plays an important part, and we're going to need all kinds of luck for this experiment to work." Quickly push off five groups of five cards, tossing them on the table.

"Now we have five poker hands. Please pick up one of the hands, look it over, and take any card from it. Please show that card to everyone but me." Take the other four cards from her and place them on top of the deck. Continue: "Place the chosen card on top of one of the other piles, and place one of the remaining piles on top."

At this point, there are three piles on the table: two five-card piles and one 11-card pile in which the chosen card lies sixth from the top. You're holding the deck.

Spread the deck out face down directly in front of Margie. As you now speak, casually straighten the piles and place the two five-card piles on top of the 11-card pile. "I'd like you to draw out one card from the deck, but don't look at it just yet. Any card at all."

After Margie draws out the card, take the deck from her and set it on the table. Pick up the combined piles and drop them on top of the deck.

"Now we're going to spell out the name of the card you just picked out. We'll deal off one card for each letter in the spelling. We'll spell out the name of the card *exactly*. For example, if you picked the queen of diamonds, we'd spell out (slowly) *queen of diamonds*. Don't worry; I'll show you how to do it."

Have her turn over the card. "Here's how you do it." Deal a card into a pile for each letter in the spelling of the card.

Leaving the pile on the table, hand her the remainder of the deck. "Now you do it."

After she spells out the name of the card, take the deck from her and place it on top of the pile you spelled out. "We'll have to get rid of some more cards," you explain. "Pick up your pile, please. Now place the top card on the bottom. Then place the next card on the table." After she does so, say, "The next one on the bottom, and the next one on the table." She continues like this until only one card remains in her hand. Stop her, making sure she doesn't turn over the card.

"What's the name of your chosen card?" She gives the name; it's the card in her hand.

Simple Speller

The first part of this trick can be done facing the spectators, but I prefer to turn my back. Ask Annette to help by shuffling the deck. Turn away and give the following instructions:

"Annette, look through the deck and find any two spot cards. Place them face up on the table, side by side. Now deal face-down cards on each one so that the total will equal ten. For instance, if you have a seven face up, you would deal a card face down on it, saying eight . . . deal another, saying nine . . . and a final card, saying ten—a total of ten. Do this for both cards." Pause.

"Notice the total of the two face-up cards. Deal that many into a separate pile from the top of the deck. Now look at the top card of the deck and show it around. That's your chosen card. Replace it on top of the deck and put the deck on the table. Pick up the pile you counted off, mix it up, and put the cards on top of the deck. You have two small piles left on the table. Turn down the face-up card in each pile. Mix the two piles together and place the cards on top of the deck."

Turn back to the group. Address Annette: "Why have I had you go through all this? Two reasons: So that you would have complete freedom of choice, and so that the position of the card in the deck would be a complete mystery to me. Therefore, we must resort to magic."

Since the trick is completely self-working, you could simply proceed. But it's best to give the spectators something extra to think about. I usually take the pack, give it one "magic riffle," and return it to my helper. All I do is riffle the ends of the deck upwards.

"I'd like you to spell out a sentence," I say, "dealing out one card for each letter. Here's the sentence: 'The next card will be yours.' "

Guide her through it. Naturally, when she finishes the spelling, you have her turn over the next card. That's it, all right.

Note

Any 22-letter sentence will work. You can improvise a sentence using the spectator's name, for instance.

Number, Please

Bill Logan invented this clever trick, which can be repeated successfully a number of times. I've simplified the calculations to make it easier for you to do the trick, and to make it *possible* for me to do it.

The effect is this: A spectator lays out cards on the table to represent a freely chosen seven-digit telephone number. Quickly gather up the cards one by one, occasionally cutting the small face-up packet. Turn the cards face down and, one at a time, *spell out* the digits in the number, moving one card from the top to the bottom for each letter in the spelling. In each instance, the last card in the spelling is turned face up and dropped on the table. Each time it's the card representing the correct digit.

Start by asking a spectator to think of any seven-digit telephone number. Have him remove cards from the deck to represent that number, laying them in a face-up row on the table. A zero would be represented by any face card, and a one by an ace. Assume that he chose the seven-digit number 651-7082. On the table he'd lay out these cards of any suits:

6   5   A   7   (face card)   8   2

Before continuing, consider this: The *value* of any card can be spelled out in three, four, or five letters. Your job is to arrange these particular cards so that they can be spelled out in order.

To start, pick up the last card in the telephone number. Pick up the 2 and place it face up in your left hand. Then pick up the second-last card. Note how many letters are in the name of the card. If the number of letters is even (four, five, nine, zero), place it on top of the card in your left hand. If the number of letters is odd (one, two, three, six, seven, eight), place it beneath the card in your left hand.

In our example, first the 2 is placed face up in the left hand. Then pick up the eight and note that it's spelled in five letters (an odd number), so place it face up *beneath* the 2.

Continue picking up cards and adding them to those in your left hand, following these rules:

Pick up the cards in reverse order.

Place each card face up on top of the face-up cards in your left hand.

Each time you do so, note how many letters are in the name of the face-up card. Divide the number of cards now in your hand *into* this number.

(1) If there's a remainder, move that number of cards from the face of the face-up pile to the bottom. (Cards may be moved singly or in a group. *Don't* count them off one on top of the other and then move them.)

(2) If there's no remainder, leave the packet as it is.

(3) Suppose the number of cards in the packet is *larger* than the number of letters in the name of the card. Simply move to the bottom of the face-up packet a number of cards equal to the number of letters in the name of the card.

Let's get back to our example. In your left hand is a face-up 2 and, below it, a face-up 8. Now continue to pick up cards in reverse order. Pick up the face card, which represents zero, and place it on those in your left hand. You now hold three cards in your left hand, and the top card, zero, is spelled in four letters. Divide 3 into 4, and you have a remainder of 1. Move one card (the face card) beneath the others.

Pick up the 7 and place it on top of the face-up packet in your left hand. This make 4 cards in the packet. The word seven is spelled in 5 letters. Divide 4 into 5, and again you have a remainder of 1. Once more, move one card from the face of the packet to the bottom.

Pick up the ace (which is considered a one) and place it on top of the pile in your left hand, bringing the total number of cards to 5. *One* has three letters. Five is greater than this, so move three cards to the bottom of the packet.

In the next two instances, the number of cards in the pile will always be greater than the number of letters in the card placed on the face of the pile. In our example, place the 5 on the packet. Since 5 is spelled in 4 letters, move four cards to the bottom of the packet.

After placing the 6 on the packet, move 3 cards to the bottom (the same number as that used in spelling 6).

Turn the packet face down. You're ready to spell out the telephone number in order. In the example, the number is

651-7082, so you first spell out 6. Move one card to the bottom, saying, "S." Move a second card to the bottom, saying, "I." Turn the third card face up, saying, "X." The card is the 6. Place it face up on the table. In the same way, spell out the 5, the 1, and then the rest of the digits in the telephone number. As you spell out the number, lay the cards out in a row, just as they were laid out at the beginning.

Notes

Practise this with several telephone numbers. The procedure is actually quite easy to remember.

At first you may have some difficulty remembering that you must consider the number of letters in the spelling of the card, and not the value of the card itself. For example, you may think of a three as having a value of three, whereas *the word* actually contains five letters. A little practice will solve the problem.

The explanation is lengthy, but this is a very fast trick which captivates spectators. Repeat it at least twice.

Nine to One

This trick was inspired by a Martin Gardner invention and a derivation by Robert Neale.

In your pocket you have a packet of nine cards. The suits are unimportant, so from the face of the packet to the top these are the values: 3, J, A, K, 7, 4, 2, J, 8. Let's assume that you're using blue-backed cards. The sixth card from the bottom, the four, will be *red-backed.*

Remove the packet from your pocket and turn it face up. Deal it out in three rows so that, as you look at them, the cards are laid out like this:

        3 J A
        K 7 4
        2 J 8

Ask Wayne to help out. "This will be a spelling test, Wayne—but a very easy one. We'll see if you can spell out the names of these cards. On the first letter, touch the card you choose to spell. Then you touch the card next to it or below it for the next letter. And so on. For instance, if you were spelling 'seven,' you might do it like this."

Touch the 7 and spell S-E-V-E-N, touching a different card for each letter in the spelling. You may touch the adjoining card on either side, or you may touch the card immediately above or below it. You may not, however, move diagonally. You may, in fact, go back the way you came and touch cards you've touched previously.

Demonstrate the spelling of seven at least twice. The second time, demonstrate how Wayne might retrace his steps and touch a card more than once.

"You may start on any card, and we'll see how many you can spell."

He spells out a card. Have him hold his finger on the one he lands on. "Let's get rid of the face cards. Which one should we turn down first?" Turn over whichever one he indicates. "This is going to get tough now, because you have to end up on a *face-up* card. Now turn over the card you landed on and then spell it out the same way as you did the first one. By the way, you can spell on a face-down card; you just can't *land* on one."

He starts with the card he landed on and spells out its value as he did before. Have him hold his finger on it. "We'd better get rid of another face card. Which one?" He tells you, and you turn it face down. Again he notes the card he landed on, turns it face down, and then spells it out.

"Now we'll get rid of that last face card," you say, turning it face down.

Wayne continues the spelling process until only one card remains face up.

"Congratulations, Wayne. You did it perfectly. Remember

now, you had complete freedom of choice as to which cards you would spell and how you would spell them. And there's only one card that you chose not to spell."

Turn the remaining card—the four—face down in place. The red back stands out among the blue-backed cards. "Well, no wonder. It doesn't fit in with all the rest."

Note

Why does this work? As I indicated, something of a mathematical principle is in operation. Cards can be spelled out in three, four, or five letters. Since some cards are spelled out with an odd number of letters and some with an even number of letters, all one need do is place the cards so that the red-backed card can never be reached by the spelling procedure. The trouble is that three other cards cannot be reached, either. Therefore, place face cards in these positions and eliminate them as the trick proceeds.

Obviously, any three- or five-letter cards can be substituted for the ones I use in the layout.

UNEXPECTED REVERSALS

Fan Out

Take any nine cards and spread them out in a face-down fan. Ask a spectator to pull out one card slightly, lift it up, and look at its name. Then your helper is to push the card back into the fan. Note the number of the card from the top of the packet. Say, "I'll mix the cards a bit." Now move cards from the top to the bottom, taking one, two, or three at a time. The object is to move the chosen card to the fifth position from the top, so you add 13 to the number of the chosen card from the top. If the original position was sixth from the top, you'd add 13 to this and move 19 cards from the top to the bottom.

Spread out the cards in a fan once more. Remove the card at the far right, turn it face up, and insert it halfway in at the second position from the left (Illus. 10). As you turn over the

Illus. 10

card, say, "I'm not sure what your card is. It could be this, or not." Say something similar as you turn over succeeding cards. Remove the card now at the far right, turn it face up, and insert it halfway in at the fourth position from the left end. Continue with the next two cards on the right, so that every other card is face up, sticking halfway out of the deck (Illus. 11).

Illus. 11

   Close up the fan and turn the pile over edgewise, the cards still sticking out of the deck. Hold the packet with both hands. Your right hand from above grips its lower portion loosely. Your left hand from below grips the upper portion (Illus. 12).

Illus. 12

With your left first finger, push down the protruding cards so that they plunge out three cards below the packet (Illus. 13).

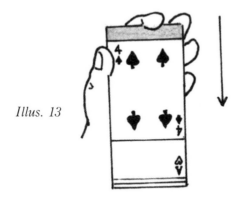

Illus. 13

Right hand not shown for clarity.

Pull these cards away from the packet with your right hand. With your left thumb, flip over the packet remaining in your left hand. Drop the cards in your right hand onto this packet. Call attention to the face-up card, saying "It might be this card." Remove the face-down card from the back of the pile. Turn it face up, saying, "But I'm pretty sure it isn't this one." Drop it face up on the face of the packet. Flip the entire pile over, saying, "There's only one way I can find out for sure. What's the name of your card?"

When the name is given, spread out the cards, showing the chosen card face up in the middle.

Over & Over

This trick requires no technical skill whatever. Have someone cut the deck into two piles which are approximately even. Your volunteer is to look at the top card of one pile, and then turn the other pile face up on it.

Take the deck and fan off several cards. Turn them over endwise on the others, turning your right hand over in the process (Illus. 14). Push off several more cards with your left

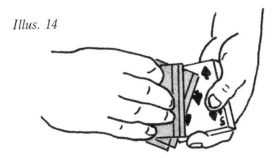

Illus. 14

thumb. Take these under the cards in your right hand. Then turn your hand back to its original position. Add cards to the bottom each time, as you continue turning your hand over and back.

When you get to the first face-down card (the chosen one), add it to the group you're currently fanning. Move your right hand away and flip over the cards in your left hand with your left thumb (Illus. 15). Bring your right hand back and

Illus. 15

add several cards from your left hand to the bottom of those in your right. Turn over your right hand and add cards to the bottom, as before. Continue until all the cards are in your right hand. Even up the cards.

The bottom portion of the deck is face up, and the top portion is face down. You may see a natural break between the two sections. If you don't, tilt the cards forward and riffle the inner edge with your right thumb until you find the break. Lift off the face-down cards with your right hand. Flip over the face-up cards with your left thumb. Place the portion that's in your right hand on top.

Ask the spectator to name the chosen card. It is the only face-up card in the face-down deck.

The sloppier you can make the shuffling, the better.

What's Up?

I came across this trick in Walter B. Gibson's 1947 book *Professional Magic for Amateurs.* I do Gibson's version, with an improvement.

Ask Vernon to help out. Shuffle the deck and cut off about two-thirds of the cards. "These are mine," you say. Hand Vernon the lower third, saying, "And the other half is for you." Turn away and continue: "Please shuffle your cards." You also shuffle yours. "Now we'll each choose a card from our pile. Kindly show your selection around and then hold it face down."

Turn away, note the bottom card of your pile and turn it face up on the bottom. Turn over the entire pile, so that the card you looked at is the lone face-down card on top of the pile. Take any other card and hold it face down in your right hand.

Ask Vernon if he's ready. Turn back, saying, "I don't want to know your card, and I don't want you to know mine." Set the card that's in your hand on the table, telling him to do the same with his card. Pick up his card and carefully slide it into your pile, about two-thirds of the way down. "Take my card and sneak it into your pile the same way."

Now you're holding all face-up cards with the exception of the top card, which you know, and the spectator's card, which you just stuck into your pile.

Casually drop your left hand to your side as you extravagantly gesture with your right hand and say, "Would you be good enough to give me your pile, please?"

You dropped your left hand with the palm up (Illus. 16). Bring your hand up with the palm *down,* back of the hand uppermost (Illus. 17). Place the spectator's pile below this pile and take the entire pack into your right hand.

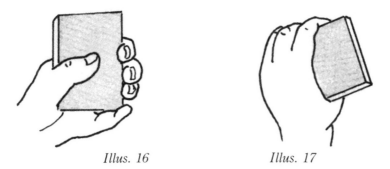

Illus. 16   *Illus. 17*

"My card was . . ." Name the card you looked at earlier. "What was the name of your card?" Repeat the names of both cards. Then spread out the deck, revealing that both are face up.

RED-&-BLACK MAGIC

The Forecast is Fair

Arthur Hill developed this prediction trick; I've added some variations.

Cecilia volunteers to help out. After she shuffles the pack, fan through the cards, noting the first black card from the bottom. Suppose it's the six of clubs. Continue fanning through the cards until you come to its mate, the six of spades. Place this card face down on the table, saying, "Here's my prediction card."

Spread the deck face down on the table, saying, "Cecilia, I'd like you to take 25 cards from the deck. Take them in bunches, or singly—whatever you wish. So you'll be sure I won't know any of the cards, don't take from too near the top or the bottom." This instruction ensures that she doesn't take that first black card from the bottom. After she's taken her cards, have her check the count. "So now you have half the deck. Well, almost half the deck. I get the extra card. After all, it's *my* trick." Gather up the remaining spread-out cards, making sure that the first black card from the bottom stays in the same position. Set your packet on the table.

"The object of this trick is to show the close relationship between the red and the black cards in the deck. I'd like you to secretly count the number of red cards that you have."

When she finishes, have her set her packet on the table. Now do your best to thoroughly confuse the onlookers. Have Cecilia cut off some cards from her pile and shuffle them. She sets these down and shuffles the remainder of her original pile. She cuts off some cards from the top of *your* pile, shuffles them, and sets them next to your original pile. In other words, she shuffles both of her piles and the top portion of your original pile.

Gather up the cards. Her two piles go on the bottom. Your unshuffled portion goes on next, and your shuffled pile goes on top.

"Now we'll find out if there's actually a relationship between the red and black cards. How many red cards did you have?" Suppose she says 12. "Let's count down to that same number of black cards." From the face-down deck, deal the cards into a face-up pile, counting aloud as you come to each black card. When you come to the twelfth black card, toss it aside face up. Gather up the cards and set the deck aside. Finally, show that your prediction card matches the one that was counted to.

Stop Sign

Roy Walton invented this location trick based on a principle similar to that used in *The Forecast Is Fair* (page 54).

Ask Doug to shuffle the pack and then deal into a face-down pile. He must deal fewer than 26. Secretly keep track of the number he deals. Subtract this number from 27. This is your key number. Suppose he's dealt 18 cards. Subtract 18 from 27, giving you 9. You must remember the number 9.

Tell Doug, "Please pick up the cards you dealt off. Fan through them and secretly count the red cards." When he's done, turn away, and continue: "Set that pile down and pick up the rest of the deck. Now you counted a certain number of red cards. I want you to look at the faces and count to that same number in *black* cards. For instance, if you counted 12 red cards, you'd count to the 12th black card from the bottom. That will be your selected card." When he's done, say, "Close up the cards and turn them face down. Place them on top of the pile on the table."

Turn back, pattering, "What we've tried to do is have a card selected completely at random. Now let's see if I can read your thoughts. Pick up the deck and slowly deal the cards, one by one, into a face-up pile. When you come to your card, I want you to *think* 'stop.' But try not to pause, hesitate, or in any way give away the position of your card. Just continue dealing at the same pace."

As he deals, count the black cards. The card that lies at your key number (in our example, the ninth black card) is the one he chose. Let him deal a card or two more and then say, "I got a strong impression a moment ago." Push the chosen card out from the others. "Is this your card?"

The One & Only

The original trick is the invention of Karl Fulves. In its effect, it is somewhat similar to *Nine to One* (page 45), but the principle is totally different.

Let's assume you're using a deck with blue backs. You're going to use 16 cards, 8 of the black suits and 8 of the red suits. The values and the specific suits don't matter. One of the red-suit cards, however, will be from a different deck and will have a *red back*. Let's say this card is the queen of hearts.

Remove the packet of 16 cards from your pocket and turn it face up. Deal the cards out face up. This is how they'll appear from the spectator's view:

B	R	R	R
R	B	B	B
R	B	QH	R
R	B	B	B

So, for you to deal the packet out in a natural order—left to right, one row below another—the cards must be set up, from the bottom of the packet, like this: B B B R, R QH B R, B B B R, R R R B.

You'll also need a marker of some sort. A mysterious-looking medal or a foreign coin is perfect. Any coin will do, however. Hand the coin to a spectator, saying, "This will aid us in an experiment to determine whether our minds are in tune. If all works out, it might be an example of coincidence . . . or it might be some mysterious form of telepathy. I'll turn my back and give you some instructions. I want you to act on impulse only. Do whatever first occurs to you. If you stop to think, it could conceivably interfere with any possible telepathic waves."

Turn away and give the following instructions, pausing after each:

"Place the coin on any *red* card—complete freedom of choice."

"Move the coin to the left or the right to the nearest black card; you may choose *either* left or right. If there's no black card to the left or right, just leave the coin where it is."

"Move the coin either up or down to the nearest red card. Again, you have the choice of going *either* up or down."

"Move the coin diagonally to the nearest black card."

"Move the coin either down—towards you—or to the right to the nearest red card."

Turn back. The coin should be resting on the queen of hearts. "Let's see if we were able to mentally communicate." Turn over, in place, all of the cards except for the queen of hearts. "All blue backs." Remove the coin from the queen of hearts and turn the card over. It is, of course, the only card with a red back.

LONG-DISTANCE CALLS

Phony Coincidence

By way of preparation, write a column of numbers, from 1 to 35, on a sheet of paper. Phone Ramona and ask her to get a deck of cards.

"Please give the cards a good shuffle, Ramona. Now it happens that I'm thinking of a particular card. I wonder if *you'd* choose the same card. Let's find out. Cut off a pile of cards. Set the rest of the deck aside. Now from the top, deal your cards into a face-up pile. Please name each card as you deal it out. Keep going until you finish the pile you cut off."

As Ramona names each card, jot down that number next to the appropriate number on your sheet. (Use this shorthand: For nine of clubs, 9C; for queens of spades, QS; for ace of hearts, AH, etc.)

When Ramona finishes naming the cards, say, "That's amazing! My card is in that group."

Your key numbers are 1, 2, 4, 8, 16, 32. Note how many cards are in Ramona's pile. *Subtract from this the next-lower key number.* Suppose the pile contained 23 cards. Subtract the next-lower key number, which is 16. 23 minus 16 is 7. Double the result, which gives you 14. Look at your sheet. The card at number 14 will be the one you're thinking of.

Say to Ramona, "Pick up your pile and turn the cards face down. Now deal the top card onto the deck and put the next one on the bottom of your pile. Put the next one on top of the deck and the next one on the bottom of your pile. Keep doing this until you have only one card left."

When she's done, say, "The card I was thinking of was . . ." Name the card you noted at number 14. Ask, "What's your card?" It's the same, of course.

A brief review of the latter part of the trick: Your helper has finished listing her cards. You note the number in the pile. Suppose the total is 14. You subtract from this the next-lower key number, which is 8. 14 minus 8 is 6. You double 6, giving you 12. The card you noted at number 12 will be the one your helper will end up with.

Are You There?

Have a pencil and paper ready. Phone a friend and ask him to get out a deck of cards. Give him the following directions:

"Shuffle the deck. Look at the bottom card and remember it. Count onto the table from the top of the deck a number equal to the value of the card you looked at. A jack counts as 11, a queen 12, and a king 13. Now place the rest of the deck on top of those cards."

When he's done, say, "Now name the cards, starting with the top card of the deck and working on down." After he names the first card, say, "Stop! I forgot something. Put that card back on top. I wanted you to cut the cards first. Cut off about half the cards and place the other half on top."

But make sure you jot down the name of the card he called out. This is your key card. After he cuts the cards, say, "Now please name the cards, starting with the top card."

As he names the cards, jot down their names, using this shorthand: AC, 9H, 2D, etc. Stop writing when the spectator calls the name of the key card. Suppose that card were the nine of diamonds. These might be the last 15 cards you jotted down:

5D 2H 7H 10H 5H 9H JS 5C AC KD JC 8H 7S 4D 9D
13 12 11 10 9 8 7 6 5 4 3 2 1 — —

Now number the cards as above. Don't put a number under your key card, nor under the card named before it.

When a number corresponds to the value of a listed card, that's the chosen card. In the example above, the chosen card is the ten of hearts. If there are two possibilities, eliminate one by naming the suit or value of one of the cards. For instance, you might say, "I get a strong feeling that your card is a club." If your assistant agrees, you have the right card. If you're wrong, name the other possibility.

Something to Sniff At

As far as I know, the original telephone trick was called *The Wizard.* Spread out the cards face up and have someone push out a card. Then dial "The Wizard," actually a confederate. When your friend answers the phone, ask, "Is The Wizard there?" Immediately the confederate begins naming the suits. Upon hearing the correct suit, you say, "Hello." Your confederate now knows the suit of the chosen card. She immediately begins naming the values, like this, "Ace, king, queen, jack, ten," etc. When she names the proper value, say, "Here," and hand the phone to the person who chose the card. The Wizard immediately tells him the name of his card.

Here we have an extremely subtle adaptation of the same trick. Again, the deck is spread out face up and a spectator pushes out a card. Dial the number of your confederate. When she answers, clear your throat. As before, she begins naming the suits. When she hits the correct suit, you sniff. She names the values. When she hits the right value, you again sniff.

Hand the phone to the spectator. Whisper to him, "Ask for your card any way you want to." When the spectator says

"Hello," your confederate says, "Hello, hello. Who's calling, please? Hello." This, of course, creates the illusion that she's just answered the phone.

The spectator asks for the name of his card and is given the correct answer.

SPECIAL ARRANGEMENTS

Easy Opener

Jay Ose often used this opening trick, I've made a few minor changes.

Remove the four aces from the deck. The ace of hearts goes on top of the deck, and the ace of diamonds goes on the bottom. The third card from the top is the ace of clubs, and the fourth card from the top is the ace of spades. Place the deck in its card case.

In performance, get a volunteer—Susie, for instance. Remove the deck from its case and set the case aside. Set the deck on the table. Make sure no one gets a peek at the bottom card.

"Susie, I'd like you to think of an ace—A-C-E, ace. It could be your favorite ace, or one you don't care for at all. Do you have an ace in mind? What is it?"

She names the ace. Suppose she names the ace of hearts. Say, "Put your hand on top of the deck and say, 'I want the top card to be the ace of hearts.' " She does so. Have her lift her hand. Turn over the top card, showing that her wish has come true.

Suppose she names the ace of diamonds. Say, "Put your hand on top of the deck and say, 'I want the bottom card to be the ace of diamonds.' " She removes her hand and you turn the deck over, showing the bottom card. Make sure that you don't inadvertently show the top card as well.

Suppose the names the ace of clubs or the ace of spades. Say, "As I said, 'Ace, A-C-E.' " Pick up the deck. Spell out A-C-E, dealing one card from the top into a pile for each letter. If she named the ace of clubs, turn over the last card you dealt. If she named the ace of spades, turn over the current top card of the deck.

In all instances, gather up the cards and give them a good shuffle, destroying all the evidence. As you do so, patter about how incredible it is that she should have thought of that very ace. Go right into your next trick.

It's in Your Hands

The spectator handles the cards throughout an "impossible" location of a chosen card.

In preparation, remove all the clubs from the deck. From top to bottom, arrange them in this order:

10   9   8   7   6   5   4   3   2   A   K   Q   J

The stack goes on the bottom of the deck, making the jack of clubs the bottom card.

In performance, set the deck face down on the table. Ask Bert to cut off a portion and shuffle it. Make sure he doesn't cut into your stack. "Replace the packet on top of the deck, please. Then take the top card, show it around, and replace it on the top."

When Bert's done, have him give the pack a complete cut. He, or someone else, gives the deck another complete cut.

Say, "Let's try something different. Turn the deck face up and give the cards a complete cut."

Have various spectators continue cutting the cards until a club shows up on the face of the deck. At this point, say, "That should be enough. The cards should be sufficiently mixed. Turn the deck face down, please."

You now know the position of the chosen card from the top. How? You add three to the value of the bottom card. Suppose a spectator has cut the six of clubs to the bottom.

Add three to six, getting nine. The chosen card is ninth from the top. The ace is figured as one.

The obvious exception is when the jack, queen, or king of clubs is cut to the face of the deck. Just consider the jack as one, the queen as two, and the king as three—which should be easy to remember. So if the jack appears on the bottom, the chosen card will be on top; if the queen is on the bottom, the chosen card will be second from the top; and if it's the king, the chosen card will be third from the top.

As before, suppose the six of clubs was on the bottom. The deck is now face down on the table, and you know the chosen card is ninth from the top.

Harry Lorayne suggested this procedure: Have the spectator place his hand on the deck. Say, "Your card is 41st from the top, so please push down on the deck. Good! It's now 25th from the top. Push down a little harder. Hold it, hold it! You now have it 9th from the top. Any more pushing and you might push it out of the deck altogether. Let's check that 9th card and see if I'm right."

Have the spectator deal off nine cards into a pile. Ask him to name his card and then to turn over the last one dealt.

Note

In the original version of this trick, the cards were stacked on the bottom in their natural order. This could give the trick away. A *five* shows up on the bottom, and the chosen card is *five* from the top. Not good.

Four of a Kind

Milt Kort called my attention to this trick; I've made a few changes in the handling.

Here's the way you make the setup. Remove from the deck all threes, sixes, sevens, nines, and fives. Actually, any five values will do, but these seem to work well in keeping the setup concealed. Mixing the suits, make a set of five which includes all five values in random order. For example, place the nine of clubs face up on the table. On top of it, face up, place the six of diamonds. Next, the five of clubs. Then the seven of spades. Last, the three of hearts. The suits don't matter so long as they're chosen randomly. From bottom to top, you now have face up on the table nine, six, five, seven, three; and the suits are mixed (Illus. 18).

Illus. 18

On top of these, place face up another set of five in exactly the same order, mixing the suits. Do this twice more. Pick up your stack and put it face down on top of the deck. Put the deck in its case, and you're ready to go.

To perform, remove the deck from the case. From the top deal twenty cards into a pile on the table, counting aloud as you do so. For our purposes, the setup is still retained. Set aside the rest of the deck.

"This little experiment has its ups and downs," you say. "Here, for example, I've dealt 20 cards *down*." Ask Johanna to assist you. "Johanna, please give the cards a complete cut." After she does so, have the cards cut at least once more—by Johanna, or by someone else.

Say to Johanna, "I'd like you to put the cards behind your back and give the packet a complete cut. As I mentioned, this experiment has its ups and downs. What I'd like you to do is turn the top card of your packet face up, and then cut the cards again." When she's done, have her bring the packet forward.

Take the cards from her, saying. "Your card is now face up. Watch how I magically cause the card to turn face down." Turn the packet face up and fan through to her face-down card. "See! There it is. Not my best work, maybe, but it's a start." Set all the cards to the right of her card face up on the table. Place her card face down on the table in a position near you. Take the remaining cards into your right hand and drop them face up onto the face-up packet on the table. You've removed her card and have managed to cut the packet at the point where her reversed card lay.

"Now we're going to find out how lucky you are. We'll need to have two equal piles." Hold the cards face down in the dealing position in your left hand. Spread out the top two cards and take them in your right hand, saying, "Two." Take the next card *under* the cards in your right hand, saying, "Three." Take the next card the same way, saying, "Four." Repeat with the next card, saying, "Five." Drop these onto the table.

Do *precisely the same thing* with the next five cards, dropping them on top of the first five. "Five and five . . . that's ten," you say.

Now form a pile to the right of the first pile. This time the counting procedure will be similar, but different. Again take the top two cards, saying, "Two." Push off the next card and, with your right thumb, draw it *on top* of the two in your right hand. As you do so, say, "Three." Draw the next card on top of those in your right hand, saying, "Four." Repeat the procedure, saying, "Five." Drop these onto the table to the right of the pile of ten.

You have four cards remaining in your hand. Take the top two in your right hand, saying, "Two." Draw the next card

on top of these with your right thumb, saying, "Three."
Repeat the procedure, saying, "Four." Drop the four cards
on top of the pile on the right. "Five and four make nine.
That's close enough. Besides, that will give us a bonus card."

Push the two piles towards Johanna. "Now I'd like you to
turn over the top card of each packet to see if the two cards
match in value." She turns over the two cards; they don't
match. "No match. Well, life has its ups and downs." Take
the two cards and set them aside *face down*. "Try again."
Once more there's no match. Take these two cards and place

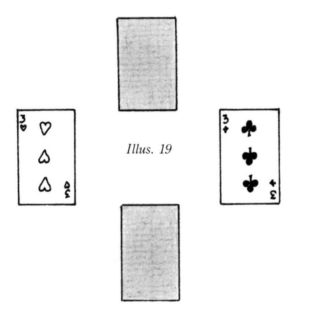

Illus. 19

them face down with the others. *Don't name the value of the
cards as she turns them over.*

Have Johanna continue. When she turns over the fifth pair,
she *has* a match. "A match! Excellent!" Take these two
cards and set them, *face up,* near the card she originally
reversed. "Now let's see if you can find any more matches."

She continues with the next four pairs without success. In each instance, turn the cards face down and toss them into the discard pile. One card remains face down on the table. Point to it, saying, "And we have our bonus card."

At this point, for visual effect, I have the four cards in a diamond formation. Nearest to me is the originally reversed card. To the right and forward of it is one of the matched cards, face up. Forming the top point of the diamond is the "bonus card," which is face down. To the left and forward of the originally reversed card is the other matched card, face up (Illus. 19).

Turn over the two face-down cards. Say, "All four match! Johanna, you may have your ups and downs, but you're *extremely* lucky."

As you speak, gather up the unmatched pairs and shuffle them into the deck.

Note

You use two different procedures in counting the nineteen cards so that the unmatched pairs will have a maximum variety, thus allaying suspicion of a setup. You immediately turn the unmatched pairs face down so that spectators will be less likely to note the repetition of specific values.

Most Magicians

This routine was originally developed by Stewart James. I like to do the J.W. Sarles version.

A simple setup is required: In a face-up pile place any six spades, other than those used in the spade royal flush. On top of these, place the ace of clubs, ace of hearts, and ace of diamonds, in any order. On top of these, in order, place the ace of spades, ten of spaces, jack of spades, queen of spades, and king of spades. Place all on top of the deck.

Sidney will assist you. Explain, "Most magicians have a card selected like this. They either fan the cards out face down." Do so. "Or they fan the cards out face up." Do so, making sure you don't fan into your setup. "But I'm not most magicians." Close up the cards and turn them face down. Address Sidney: "I'd like you to give me a number between 10 and 20." He gives you the number. You deal that many cards into a face-down pile onto the table.

Tap the last card dealt. "Most magicians would have you take this card. But I'm not most magicians." Set the rest of the deck aside for the moment. Pick up the pile you just dealt. Let's suppose Sidney chose the number 15. "You had me deal out 15 cards. The digits are 1 and 5. Let's add them together. What do we get?" He replies. "Right, 6." Deal six cards into a pile. Tap the last card you dealt and avert your head. "I'd like you to look at this card and show it around. Then replace it on top of the pile."

When he's done, place the pile in your hand on top of the pile on the table. Pick up the combined pile. "Let's mix these up a bit," you say. Remember the number the spectator chose? Now transfer that number of cards from the top to the bottom of the pile, moving one, two, or three cards each time. At the end of this "shuffle," the packet will be in precisely the same order. As you transfer cards, silently keep track. In our example, move 15 cards and then quit. "That should do it," you declare. Place the packet on top of the deck.

Spread out some of the top cards, saying, "Most magicians would fan through the deck and find your card. But . . ." At this point, you can either pantomime the rest of the statement, or let the audience complete it for you. Say, "Instead, I'm going to see if the deck will tell me what your card is." Hold the deck to your ear and thoughtfully riffle the edges. Gradually you reveal that the card is black, a spade, the ace of spades. For each revelation, give the cards a little riffle.

Bring the deck forward and give a satisfied smile. Spectators will assume you're done.

Continue: "*Most* magicians would consider that enough. But . . ." Pause a moment, pointing your thumbs towards yourself. "Your card is the ace of spaces. Let's spell *ace*." Spell *ace,* into a pile one card for each letter in the spelling. "Now, *spades*." To the right of the first pile, spell out *spades* in the same way. Turn over the top card of the deck. It's the ace of spades. Set the ace of spades face up beyond the two piles on the table.

Again, smile and give a little nod, as though you're done. Pause. Then say, "*Most* magicians . . ." You need not say any more. Point to the three-card pile on the table. "Here we have the ace pile." Turn the cards over, showing the three aces. "And here we have the spades pile." Turn over the other pile, showing the six spades.

"Thank you, thank you," you say, taking a little bow. Pause.

"*Most* magicians . . ." Pause. "But we're not quite done," you say. "We have the ace of spades, and we'll require four more cards to make a poker hand." Deal off four cards from the top into a face-down pile. Now turn these cards over one by one, setting them in a row next to the ace of spades. As you do so, say, "*Most* magicians would quit right now. And so will I . . . because you can't beat a royal flush in spades."

Cutting the Aces

Wally Wilson dazzled me with this trick. I have no idea who originated the effect, which is a clever adaptation of an old principle.

A simple setup is necessary. Collect the four aces and arrange them, along with two other cards, like this: Place an ace face up on the table. On top of this place another ace face up. The next card—any card but an ace—is also face up. On this place any card but an ace *face down*. And, on top of all, two face-down aces. So, from the top down, you have three face-down cards (ace, ace, any card), followed by three face-up cards (any card, ace, ace) (Illus. 20). Place the whole stack on top of the deck.

Ready? Ask a spectator to help you. "As I riffle these cards, please stick your finger in wherever you wish." Hold the deck in the dealing position in your left hand. With your

Two aces

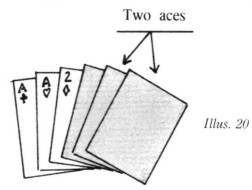

Illus. 20

right fingers, riffle the outer end of the deck from the bottom up, going as slowly as you can (Illus. 21). After the spectator inserts his finger, lift off the upper portion with your right hand, allowing withdrawal of his finger. Turn this packet over sideways and place it face up onto the cards in your left hand, saying, "We'll mark the exact spot you chose."

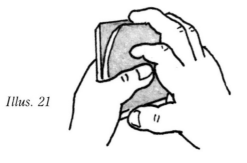

Illus. 21

Even up all the cards. Ask: "And where's the card you selected?" Fan through the pack to the first face-down card. Lift the face-up cards with your right hand. With your left thumb, push off the first face-down card so that it drops to the table, still face down.

Turn over the cards in your right hand *end for end* and place them beneath those in your left hand (Illus. 22).

Illus. 22

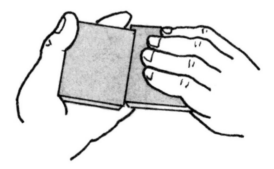

Repeat the entire maneuver, starting with riffling the outer ends of the cards for the insertion of the spectator's finger. The business is performed four times in all.

At the end, you say, "Let's see which cards you selected." Turn the aces face up one by one.

Note

You'll end up with a face-up card in the deck. If you don't have an opportunity to secretly turn the card over, simply proceed with other tricks. What with various spectators shuffling the deck, it's not unusual that a card should turn out to be face up. When it's noticed, simply say, "No wonder I'm having so much trouble. We've got a face-up card here." Then turn the card over.

"Guts" Poker

U.F. Grant developed a brief poker demonstration. The demonstration should be done while seated at a table.

To start, you must have the four aces on top of the deck. Casually give the deck a few riffle-shuffles, keeping the four aces on top.

Explain, "Card sharps usually win, not by cheating, but because they know the odds. Sometimes they resort to cheating. But I've discovered that you don't have to know the odds and you don't have to cheat—*if* you're very lucky. And I happen to be very lucky. Let me demonstrate."

Ask Woody, who's seated opposite you, to help out. Set the deck down and ask the person seated to your right to cut the cards. After he picks a packet from the top, pick up the lower portion and begin dealing. This is a fairly normal procedure in informal games. The person who cut the cards will place his portion on the table.

Deal two poker hands in the normal manner—one to Woody and one to yourself. "This will be a wide-open game," you say. "You may draw as many cards as you want. But not more than five . . . if you don't mind."

You're still holding the packet you dealt from. "How many cards do you want?" He tosses some cards aside, and you deal him the same number. Then casually set the remaining cards down *to the right* of the other packet on the table (Illus. 23). Pick up your hand and study it, murmuring something

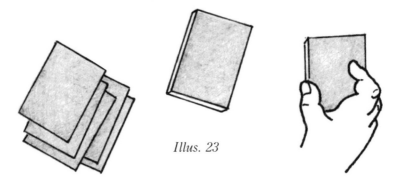

Illus. 23

like, "I seem to have run out of luck. This is the worst hand I've *ever* held." The point is to kill a little time, giving on-lookers a chance to forget which packet is which. Finally discard four cards from your hand. "I guess I'll take four."

Pick up the pile which was originally the top section and deal yourself four cards—the aces, of course. Place the re-maining cards on top of the packet on the table.

Do some imaginary betting with Woody, then ask him to show his hand. "As I mentioned, you don't have to be skill-ful—if you're lucky."

Turn over your cards one at a time.

ALL IN THE MIND

You Might Wonder

You might wonder why a trick this simple would work. After the deck is shuffled by a spectator, take the cards back. Comment that you need a prediction card as you fan through the deck, faces towards yourself. At first, fan rapidly through the cards, noting the top card. Then fan through more slowly, looking for the mate to the top card—the one that matches it in color and value. Remove that card and set it aside, face down, announcing that it's your prediction.

Hand the deck face down to Ernie, saying, "Please deal the cards one at a time into a face-down pile." After he's dealt 15 cards or so, say, "You may stop any time you wish." When he stops, take the remainder of the cards from him and set them aside.

Tell him, "Pick up the pile you dealt and turn it face up. Now deal those into a *face-up* pile and stop whenever you wish." Again, when he stops, take the cards remaining in his hand and set them aside. Say, "Pick up the pile, turn it face down, and deal as many as you wish."

He stops; you take the remaining cards and set them aside. He continues, alternately dealing from a face-up packet and a face-down packet, until only one card remains. Take this card and set it next to your prediction card. If the card is face up, simply turn over your prediction card, showing the match. If the card is face down, turn over the two cards simultaneously.

Note
Make sure that the top card isn't an obvious one, like an ace or face card. On every other deal, the "chosen" card is

briefly displayed, so it should be a spot card, which is unlikely to be noted. If the top card is an ace or face card, have a spectator give the cards an additional shuffle.

Good Companions

This trick was invented by Roy Walton. Openly remove ten matching pairs from the deck—that is, two nines, two threes, two fives, etc. Take only one pair of each value; for instance, don't take two pairs of nines. As you remove the pairs, place them in a face-up pile. Turn the pile face down. While removing the pairs, explain, "I'm removing ten pairs of matching cards to try an experiment. If it works, you'll see a demonstration of my mental powers. If not, you'll see a demonstration of my total humiliation."

Now perform a deceptive maneuver. In a casual overhand shuffle, draw off any *even* number of cards singly from the top. Drop the rest of the packet on top of these. You may repeat the maneuver a few times.

Deal the packet into two face-down piles, alternating the placement of the cards. Put one pile on top of the other. Now you'll need two assistants.

Give the cards a complete cut. Ask Spectator 1 to do the same. And ask Spectator 2 to also give the packet a complete cut. This makes three cuts in all, and three, of course, is a mystical number.

Deal the packet into two piles, alternating as before. Give one pile to Spectator 1 and the other to Spectator 2.

Tell Spectator 1, "Give your pile a complete cut. And you may give it another, if you wish. Now remove *either* the top or bottom card and, without looking at it, set it face down to one side." Give Spectator 2 the same instructions, only he sets his selection face down on top of Spectator 1's card.

Address Spectator 1 again: "Please deal your remaining nine cards into a face-down row. You may deal from left to right or from right to left. You may deal with your packet face up or face down. But if you deal with the packet face up, deal the cards face down because I don't want to see any of the cards." If he decides to deal with the packet face up, avert your head while he deals.

Spectator 2 is given the same instructions, except that he is to deal his cards face down on top of Spectator 1's cards. He may also start at either end and deal with the packet face up or face down.

When they're finished, you say, "Each of you selected a card completely at random. You cut your packet and selected either the top or bottom card. There's no way I could control your choice, right? And you had complete freedom in dealing out your cards in a row. Let's see what I can do."

Slowly pass your hand over the row of cards, trying to get a vibration. The second time you pass your hand over, it quivers a bit as you reach the center pair, but you continue on without pausing. Eventually, you'll choose the middle pair, the fifth pair from either end. Again you pass your hand over the row and your hand trembles visibly as it passes the middle pair. At length, you pass your hand very slowly over the cards and your hand trembles violently at the middle pair, so you drop it on top of these cards. "I get a strong vibration right here," you say. Turn over the pair, showing the cards and naming them. Turn over the originally selected pair. They are the exact mates to the ones you selected.

You can turn the other pairs face up as you gather them up. There's no evidence whatever of how you did it.

Lie Like a Rug

Jack Vosburgh invented this trick.

Before you begin, sneak a peek at the top card of the deck. Then you'll need the assistance of three spectators.

Set the deck on the table and ask one of the spectators to cut the cards into three piles. Each of the spectators now chooses a pile and takes the top card from it. Your job is to note which of the three takes the card that you know.

Explain, "This is an informal lie detector test. Over the years I've acquired the ability to tell if someone is lying. Let's test it out. In a moment, I'd like the three of you to decide which one of you will tell the truth about the card he selected. So *one* of you will be a truth-teller. The other two should name each other's card."

Make sure all is understood, then turn away while the three make their decision. When you turn back, ask each spectator in turn which card he took. Then point to one spectator, saying, "You're lying." Point to a second spectator and repeat the accusation. Point to the third spectator, saying, "Congratulations! *You* are a truth-teller."

How do you know? Simple. If the person who took the card you peeked at names that card, the other two are liars. If he names some other card, then he is one of the liars; the other liar is the one who names the card you peeked at.

Hopelessly Lost

There's apparently no way in the world a chosen card can be located. Yet you manage to find it.

Before you begin, peek at the top card and remember it; this is your key card. Fan the pack out face down and have Phyllis remove a group of cards from the middle. Set the rest of the deck down. Take the packet from Phyllis, saying, "I'd like you to *think* of one of these cards as I fan them out." Avert your head. "I won't watch your face." Of course you won't; you'll be too busy silently *counting* the cards as you slowly fan the faces of the cards for Phyllis's perusal.

After she's thought of one, hand her the packet. Turn away, saying, "Please remove your card and show it to everyone. Then place it face down on the table. Shuffle the rest of the packet and put that group on top of the deck. Now put your card on top."

You could continue giving directions with your back to the group. I usually find it best to turn back at this point to make sure my directions are followed exactly. Say, "Cut off about two-thirds of the deck, please. Set that group on the table. Take the remaining third and give those cards a good shuffle. Place them on top of the deck. Obviously, your card is hopelessly lost. Still, give the deck a complete cut."

The pack may be given additional complete cuts. Take the deck and turn it face up. Continue: "Let's see if I can pick up your mental vibrations. I'll fan through the deck and, when you see your card, I'd like you to think the word *stop*. I won't watch your face because I don't want to get any physical signals." What a nice person you are! Of course the main reason you won't watch her face is that you'll be looking for your key card. When you see it, begin silently counting with the *next* card. Count the number that was in Phyllis's packet, and the last card you count is the one chosen.

Slow down as you near the end of the count, saying something like this: "I'm getting an exceptionally strong signal. Your card must be somewhere near. Perhaps I passed it. No! This is it, right here!"

Perfectly Mental

In many respects, this trick is a perfect demonstration of mind reading. A card is *freely* chosen and returned to the deck. The spectator immediately *shuffles* the deck. Nevertheless, the mentalist finds the card.

Every so often, the trick will misfire. If there is such a thing as telepathy, isn't it logical that occasionally the mentalist will get the wrong signal?

Start by getting a peek at the bottom card. This is your key card. You may give the pack a riffle shuffle, keeping the card on the bottom. Set the deck on the table and ask Leah to cut off a portion of the cards and set them on the table. Say, "Please take the card you cut to and show it around, but don't let me get a look at it." When she's done, point to the portion she cut off, saying, "Replace your card here and then put the rest of the deck on top." After she does so, say, "Now give the cards a good shuffle."

If she gives the deck one shuffle, say, "And another." Chances are, however, she'll give the cards two or three shuffles on her own. It doesn't matter whether she gives the pack riffle-shuffles, overhand shuffles, or a combination.

Take back the deck, saying, "I'd like you all to mentally picture the chosen card. Maybe this will help me discover which one it is." With an expression of deep concentration, fan through the cards, faces towards yourself. Watch for your key card. The one just preceding it is *probably* the chosen card. Tentatively pull this card from the deck, shaking your head. "I don't get *strong* vibrations, but this *might* be your card." Set the card face down on the table. Ask Leah to name her selection. If you get it right, nod, and turn the card over. If not, replace the card in the deck, saying, "Yes, I was afraid of that." Follow up with a sure-fire mental trick.

Notes

It's possible that the chosen card could be separated from your key card by one, two, or three cards. Some prefer asking probing questions to see if this is what's happened. When this is the case, the mentalist is often able to come up with the chosen card—eventually. I prefer the straightforward method, even though there's a minor risk of failure.

You can make this trick almost a certainty by using *two* easily remembered key cards, like the two black aces. Beforehand, for example, you might place the ace of clubs on top of the deck and the ace of spades on the bottom. Proceed as described above.

When you fan through the deck and find a single card between the two aces, you can be quite confident that's the one chosen. But suppose the black aces are separated. In all likelihood, the chosen card is the one preceding the ace of spades or the one after the ace of clubs. To discover which, ask a question to distinguish the two possibilities, like, "Was it a face card?" or "Was it a red card?" or "Did it have a very low value?"

As with the version using one key card, reveal your choice in a very tentative manner, leaving yourself an excuse for a possible failure.

Mystic Prediction

This is a Martin Gardner principle with a Henry Christ twist. This is my variation.

Have Don shuffle the deck. Take it back, saying, "I'll attempt to predict the future, so I'll need to find a card that will match one that you'll choose by chance."

Fan through the cards, faces towards yourself. Explain: "Notice that I don't change the position of any cards as I look for a good prediction." Note the *eighth* card from the bottom. Find its mate in the deck—that is, the card that matches it in value and color. For instance, if the eighth card from the bottom were the queen of clubs, you'd find the queen of spades. Remove this mate and place it face down on the table. Announce, "This is my prediction card." If the mate should be one of the first seven cards from the face of the deck, have the cards reshuffled. "No card stands out in my mind; maybe you should give them another shuffle," you say.

Hand the pack to Don. "We're going to have you choose a card using a random mathematical procedure. I'll describe the method that seems to work best for this experiment. Deal the top card of the deck face up, saying 'Ten' aloud. Then deal the next card face up on top of it, saying, 'Nine.' Continue down to one, or until you hit a match. Suppose you hit a six when you say 'Six' aloud. That would be a match, so you'd stop dealing in the pile. Then you'd begin another pile, again starting with ten. If you should get all the way down to one without a match, then you 'kill' that pile by placing a face-down card on top of it. In your counting, an ace is considered a one. And only tens count as ten; face cards don't.

"Undoubtedly you've heard that three, seven, or thirteen are mystic numbers. True enough. But for precognition, *four* is the critical number. So we'll need exactly four piles."

Guide Don through the process. Each time he hits a match as he counts backwards from ten, have him stop and start a new pile. If he deals out ten cards without a match, have him place a card face down on the pile, "killing" it.

After he has dealt four piles, gather up the "dead" piles, turning over the top card of each so that all the cards face the same way. Have Don shuffle this packet of "dead" piles. He places the entire packet beneath the pile from which he's been dealing.

Don adds up the cards on the face of the remaining packets. For example, if two packets remain, and the last cards dealt on these packets were 9 and 7, you'd get 16. "You have 16. Please deal 16 cards into a face-down pile."

Take the last card he deals and, without looking at it, place it face down next to your prediction card. "Let's see if my prediction worked out. If it did, these two cards should match in value and color." Turn over the two simultaneously.

Notes

This trick is actually enhanced by a repetition or two.

In the unlikely event that all four piles are "dead," simply gather up all the cards and start the trick over from the beginning.

As mentioned, after the spectator has dealt four piles, gather up the "dead" piles, righting the top card of each. The spectator shuffles these together and places the stack *on the bottom* of the cards he has left. The reason: If you don't do this, a repetition will reveal that the chosen card is always eighth from the bottom.

The Bamboozler

Get a peek at the top card of the deck. Give the cards a riffle-shuffle, keeping it on top. Set the deck down on the table. Ask Megan to cut off a pile, gesturing to show that she is to place the top portion nearer herself. Tap the card which she cut to, saying, "This card will tell me . . ." Point to the top card of the pile nearer her, continuing, ". . . what that card is."

Lift off the card she cut to, look at it, *remember it,* and replace it. Make sure no one else can see its face. "Your card is—" Name the card you peeked at originally. Have her turn the card over. You're right, of course. *Toss this card aside face up.*

Place the packet nearer you on top of the other packet. Once more you know the top card of the deck and are ready for a repeat. But *not* until you blather for a moment.

"That always seems to work the first time I try it," you might say, "but the second time is almost impossible. But I have to try; otherwise, you might think it was mere coincidence."

Repeat the trick, again discarding the named card face up. Replace your pile on top of Megan's. Again you know the top card.

"This last time I'm going to attempt something even more difficult. I'm going to name *both* cards," you say.

Suppose the card now on top of the deck is the ace of clubs. Megan again cuts off a pile. Tap the card she cut to, saying, "This is the ace of clubs." Lift off the card and look at it. Suppose it's the three of hearts. Nod your head and say, "Good."

Tap the top card of Megan's pile. "And this is the three of hearts." Lift the card off and hold it next to the actual three of hearts, making sure no one can see the faces of the cards (Illus. 24). "Oh-oh!" You appear disappointed as you see what the second card is. "I can't believe this."

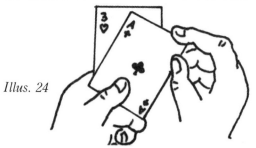

Illus. 24

Pause, shaking your head. "Ace of clubs and three of hearts." Take one of the cards into your right hand. Turn your hands over and simultaneously drop the two cards face up onto the table. This maneuver masks their original position in your hand.

Note
This trick is definitely a "quickie"; don't dawdle.

The Hocus-Pocus Pairs

Remove from the deck any A, K, Q, J, and 10, placing the cards face up in a neat pile on the table. But don't remove the cards in their natural order. You want to create the notion that the selection is random. You might, for example, remove the cards in this order: 10, Q, A, J, K. Remove another set of five cards to match these exactly. In other words, take out another 10, Q, A, J, and K. These are placed, one at a time, on top of the first set. When the packet is turned face down, the cards will be, from the top down, 10, Q, A, J, K, 10, Q, A, J, K.

While doing this, explain, "I need fairly high cards for this experiment. Somehow or other, it always seems to work better with high cards. Maybe higher cards have more power—I don't know."

Pick up the packet and turn it face down. Hold the cards in your left hand as though about to perform an overhand shuffle (Illus. 25). Lift some cards from the bottom with your right hand and drop these on top. Do this several times rapidly, as

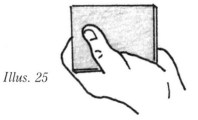

Illus. 25

though shuffling. Actually, you're merely giving the packet complete cuts. The action should be performed casually as you continue chatting. Set the packet on the table and have spectators give it several complete cuts.

"We have ten cards here." Deal five cards into a pile, saying, "One, two, three, four, five." Fan out the remaining cards, saying, "And five more." Close up the fan and place this pile next to the other. You now have two piles on the table. One pile is in reverse order to the other. The first pile, for instance, might be in this order: A, J, K, 10, Q. If so, the second pile will be in this order: Q, 10, K, J, A.

Request Rosemary's help. "What brings about a miraculous result?" you ask. "The occult? Coincidence? We seldom know. Let's eliminate all but *two cards* and see if these two will match. We'll start by giving you a choice of two words which might bring about a miraculous result. An astonishing result might be caused by *telepathy* or *luck*. Choose one of those: *telepathy* or *luck*."

Rosemary selects one of the words.

Ask her: "Pick up either pile and spell that word, transferring one card from the top to the bottom for each letter in the spelling. You need not stick with one pile. You can spell a few from one and then a few from the other—any way you want to do it—just so you spell the word correctly."

When she's done, take the top card from each pile. Put them together and set them aside face down. "There. We've eliminated one pair. Now you have another choice to make. A miracle could be brought about through *E.S.P.* or *fortune*. Choose one of those please."

After she chooses, have her spell out her choice, transferring cards from top to bottom, just as she did before. Again make it clear that she may switch piles at random as she does the spelling. When she finishes, set the top card of each pile aside as a pair, just as before. Say, "Another pair eliminated."

"You're now down to three cards in each pile. Time for another choice. An apparent miracle might be caused by *magic* or by *accident.* Choose either *magic* or *accident.* Choose one and spell it out."

As before, when Rosemary finishes, set the top two cards aside as a pair.

"And again a choice. Is a miraculous result brought about by *sorcery* or *skill?* Please pick one and spell it out."

When she finishes, take the top two cards and set them aside as a pair, saying, "So we've eliminated the last pair. Only two cards are left. You've had several choices in eliminating the various pairs. Wouldn't it be an amazing coincidence if these two cards should match?"

Turn the two cards over, showing the match. Pause for a moment, as though through with the trick. "That may be coincidence, Rosemary, but let's see if you really have *the power.*"

Turn over each of the other pairs, showing the other four matches.

Notes

For the trick to work, the exact words must be used each time. You might choose to carry a calling card on which you have the four pairs of words listed. At the appropriate time, take out the calling card, saying, "This experiment won't work unless we use the appropriate magical words." I prefer to have the "magical words" memorized.

Prediction Plus

John Bannon came up with a great idea, and J.K. Hartman improved on it. My variation eliminates all sleights.

Have a spectator shuffle the deck. Take the cards back and start fanning through them, faces towards yourself. As you do so, note the bottom card. You're looking for the three cards of the same value.

"I need to make up a prediction packet," you explain. "So I have to find three special cards." Suppose the bottom card is the two of hearts: you are seeking the other three twos. Very deliberately move the three twos, one by one, to the bottom of the deck. Naturally, you don't let anyone see the faces of the cards. Close up the deck. Then spread out five or six cards at the face of the deck. Nod your head and say, "All right."

Still keeping the cards facing you, place the tips of your right fingers beneath the fourth card from the bottom (Illus. 26). Look directly at the spectators and say with a smile, "I

Illus. 26

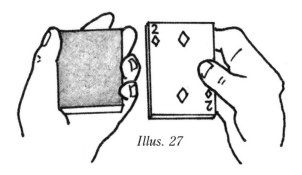

Illus. 27

have my prediction; now someone else has to do some work." As you speak, close up the cards, picking off the four twos in a packet with your right hand. Make sure that the spectators don't see the card on the face of the packet (Illus. 27). Immediately hand the deck to Oliver, saying, "Please shuffle the cards."

Through this next phase, continue holding your prediction packet exactly as you removed it from the deck—with its back to the spectators (Illus. 28).

Illus. 28

When Oliver is sure the cards are thoroughly mixed, have him hold the deck face down and deal cards one at a time into a face-down pile. Tell him: "Stop whenever you wish." When he stops, say, "Are you sure you want to stop there? You may deal more if you wish." If he deals more, repeat the offer. When he's completely satisfied, have him place the packet in his hand next to the pile he dealt off.

Ask: "Could I possibly know the top card of either pile? If you think I could, please deal some more." He's satisfied at last. "Now your chosen card is the top card of one of these piles. Point to the pile you want."

Illus. 29

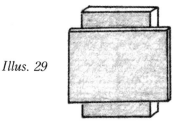

Oliver points to one of the piles. Place your prediction pile *crosswise* on this pile (Illus. 29). *"This* is the pile you chose." Immediately pick up the other pile and spread the cards out so that spectators can see the faces. Say, "You could have equally well chosen this pile and—as a matter of fact—any one of these cards." Set the pile aside.

"But you chose this pile." Pick up the pile with your right hand, casually aligning the prediction packet with the rest of the cards. Transfer the cards to the left hand. Deliberately deal off the top three cards, saying, "My prediction packet." Pause. Turn the next card face up, saying, "And your chosen card—the two of hearts." Toss it face up onto the table. Set aside the rest of the pile.

Pick up your prediction packet. One by one, turn over the other three twos, dealing them in a face-up row next to the chosen card.

Note

The timing in this trick is critical. Perform the trick exactly as described.

What's on Your Mind?

This trick once more displays your ability to read minds.

Before you start, conceal three cards in your pocket, faces inward. Agatha probably know how to shuffle, so give her a chance. Take the cards back and deal the top four cards onto the table. (Since you're going to memorize the cards, make sure you don't have two of the same value. Simply discard as unsuitable a card that matches another in value.)

"While I look away," you say, "I'd like you merely to *think* of one of these cards."

When she's done, gather up the cards, remembering their value from top to bottom. Suppose the cards are nine, jack, three, five. Simply repeat this to yourself several times.

Place the cards, face inward, into your pocket, on top of the three already there. Tell Agatha, "Please concentrate on your card."

Reach into your pocket and pull out one of the three cards you originally placed there. Don't let anyone see its face. After studying it for a moment, shake your head, and place it in the middle of the deck. Do the same with the other two cards you'd previously placed in your pocket.

Return your hand to your pocket. Ask: "What was your card?" Separate the cards so you can quickly grasp whichever is named. Produce that card.

You might try a repeat; after all, you still have three cards in your pocket.

ASSORTED DANDIES

Weight for Me

Attending a local carnival, I noticed that many were fascinated by the man who tried to guess a person's weight and age. I thought this theme might make for an amusing card trick.

"Did you ever have someone try to guess your weight?" you ask the group, as you try to generate a bit of enthusiasm for your next trick. "At a carnival, the man guarantees he can guess within three pounds. I guarantee that I can guess it exactly."

Ask Penelope to assist you. Hand her the deck and ask her to shuffle. Explain to her, "I won't necessarily guess what *you* weigh, but I will try to guess a weight that you choose. It may or may not be your weight."

Take the deck back and continue: "I'd like you to think of a weight from 100 pounds to 150 pounds, and I'll try to pick out cards to match it. But please don't pick out a weight with a zero in it, since there is no card numbered zero. Also, to make it more challenging, make sure you have *three different digits* in the weight you choose." Suppose you decide on 149 pounds. No zeros. Three different digits. You'd deal the cards like this."

To your right deal one card, saying, "This one card stands for one hundred pounds." To the left of that deal four cards, counting aloud as you do so. "These four cards stand for forty." To the left of that deal nine cards, counting aloud, and say, "These nine stand for nine pounds." Touch the piles from right to left as you say, "One hundred . . . forty . . . nine." Set the deck on the table.

"Now my back will be turned while you're dealing, but

make sure you deal quietly so that I won't have any idea of the number. When you've finished dealing, I want you to put your hands over the last two piles you dealt so that I won't be able to tell the number." Demonstrate by placing your hands on the second and third piles you dealt so that the cards are concealed.

"I'll try to match the weight you're thinking of by removing three cards from the deck. For 149, I would remove an ace, a 4, and a 9. *If* I guess right."

As you continue speaking, gather the piles one on top of the other. Tap them edgewise on the table to even them up, noting the bottom card. Put the collected cards on top of the deck. (You now know the 14th card from the top of the deck, your key card.) Make sure everything is clear to Penelope, and then hand her the deck. Immediately say, "Start dealing now," to keep her from casually shuffling. *Then* turn away.

When she finishes, turn back, and take the remainder of the deck from her. Point to the first card on your right. "This one's going to be tough," you say. Fan through the cards, faces towards you, pick out an ace, and place it face down in front of the single card.

Murmur about the difficulty of the task as you fan through the cards, pausing here and there. When you get near the top, note the number at which your key card lies from the top. This is easily done by simply counting from the key card to the top. Suppose the key card is eighth from the top. You subtract eight from *thirteen,* giving you five. In this instance, five is your *key number.*

Using this *key number* (and I'll soon explain precisely how you use it), along with an elimination process, you now select cards to place face down in front of Penelope's other two piles. After you place the two cards down, close up the deck, and *continue holding the deck face up in your left hand.*

"You can lift your hands now," you announce.

Turn over your ace, showing that you've matched the first

card. Ask how many are in the second pile. Turn over the card you placed in front of it, showing another match. Do the same with the third pile. Suppose she'd chosen the number 123. Touch each of your prediction cards, saying, "One, two, three. One hundred twenty-three. The exact weight chosen by the lady."

As you continue to speak, place your three prediction cards on the face of the deck, which is still face up in your left hand. Chat about giving it another try as you casually turn the deck face down. Continue chatting as, with your right hand, you gather the cards used by Penelope and drop them on top of the deck. You're now ready to repeat the trick, for your key card is again 14th from the top of the deck.

Using the Key Number

As you use the key number to figure out which weight was chosen, you must make certain calculations. When you're first learning the trick, this could take several seconds. *The pauses actually enhance the trick!* After all, you're supposed to be concentrating as you attempt to receive a telepathic message from the spectator.

Obviously, since the first digit will always be 1, you need only concern yourself with the other two digits. In two ways, you've limited the possible choices: There can be no number with a zero in it, and the three digits should be different.

These two eliminate 29 numbers, including all the numbers from 100 to 122. The spectator actually has a choice of only 21 numbers. (The number 149 is a special case, as I'll explain later.)

Since the first number is always 1, here are the possibilities for the last two digits:

Key Number	Possibilities
5	23 or 32
6	24 or 42
7	25 or 34 or 43
8	26 or 35
9	27 or 36 or 45
10	28 or 37 or 46
11	29 or 38 or 47
12	39 or 48

It's easy enough to figure out the possibilities. Looking at the chart, you can see that when the key number is 5 to 11, you first consider a number in the 20s; only with number 12 do you start with a number in the 30s.

Let's try several examples. The key number is 5. So you consider the possibility that the first digit may be 2, which means the second digit will be 3. So the number *could* be 23. You move up to numbers in the 30s. The first digit might be 3, in which case the second digit will be 2. You move up to the 40s. Could the number be 41? No, because the first digit in the original three-digit must be a 1, and the 1 at the end would be a duplication. So the chosen digits are either 23 or 32.

Suppose the key number is 6. Again you start with the 20s. So 24 is a possibility. Move up to the 30s. Is 33 possible? No, because that would be a duplicate of digits. Move up to the 40s. 42 is the other possibility. So the chosen digits are either 24 or 42.

Suppose the key number is 9. You start with the 20s. The number could be 27. In the 30s, the number could be 36. In the 40s, the number could be 45. So the chosen digits are 27, 36, or 45.

Using a similar process, use the key number to arrive at the possibilities. With a bit of practice, this can be done in a few seconds.

How do you discover the *exact* two-digit number? By probing. You'll never do more than two probes, and you'll never have more than one negative answer. Here are the rules I follow:

When the key number is *odd,* I say, "The weight you chose is an odd number, isn't it?" When the key number is *even,* I say, "The weight you chose is an even number, isn't it?" Whatever the answer, you now know whether the weight is odd or even.

When the Key Number Is Odd

Let's suppose that the key number is odd. You say, "The weight you chose is an odd number, isn't it?" The spectator says yes. Here are the possibilities:

Key Number	Possibilities
5	23
7	25 or 43
9	27 or 45
11	29 or 47

When the key number is 5, you know the weight immediately. Otherwise, point to the hand covering the middle pile and say, "This pile contains more cards than the other pile, right?" Whatever Penelope answers, you now know the weight.

Suppose the key number is odd, and the answer is no, the spectator didn't choose an odd number. Here are the possibilities:

Key Number	Possibilities
5	32
7	34
9	36
11	38

With just one negative answer, you know precisely the weight chosen.

When the Key Number Is Even

Your key number is even, and you've just asked the spectator, "The weight you chose is an even number, isn't it?" The spectator answers yes. Here are the possibilities:

Key Number	Possibilities
6	24 or 42
8	26
10	28 or 46
12	48

When the key number is 8 or 12, you know the correct weight immediately. Otherwise, as before, point to the middle pile and say, "This pile contains more cards than the other pile, right?"

Suppose the key number is even, and the answer is no. Here are the possibilities:

Key Number	Possibilities
8	35
10	37
12	39

Again, with only one negative answer, you know the correct weight.

Obviously, there are other (perhaps superior) ways in which you can probe. I like this method because in 8 of the 20 possibilities, you won't get a "no" answer. In the other 12 possibilities, you'll get only one negative.

You can increase the number of times you don't get a "no" answer to 10 in 20 by using a special method when the key number is 5 or 6. Suppose that the key number is 5. You don't ask whether the number is odd. Instead, remove a 2 and a 3 from the deck. Hold them fanned and say to the spectator, "I can't get it. Which of your hands is covering the higher number?" When he or she indicates which hand, place the 3 in front of that pile and the 2 in front of the other.

When the key number is 6, you don't ask whether the number is even. Instead, remove a 4 and a 2 and hold them fanned. Ask which hand is covering the higher number. Place the two cards down in the appropriate spots.

Notes

Sometimes a spectator will attempt to fool you by choosing 149 as the weight. When this is the case, you'll note that your key card is missing; it has become the top card of the third pile dealt by the spectator. After you've placed down your ace, 4 and 9, turn over the ace. Before turning over the second card, have the spectator count out pile two; then have him count out pile three. The key card is now at the bottom of the third pile. When you pick the piles up to place them on top of the deck, make sure this is the bottom pile. The key card is once more 14th from the top, and you're ready to repeat the trick.

The description above indicates that you more or less ask direct questions of the spectator. Actually, you must proceed with all sorts of telepathic mumbo-jumbo. Pass your hand over the two critical piles, searching for appropriate vibrations. "I get a strong feeling that . . ." "Somehow I get the impression that . . ." "Could I be wrong about this? I get really mixed vibrations. Is it possible that . . ."

The Lonely Pair

This classic trick requires no sleights.

The effect is that a spectator blindly chooses one pair from a great many pairs. It turns out that she's chosen the only matched pair in the bunch.

Fan through the deck, faces towards you, saying to Dolores, "I have to get some good cards for you to choose from." Remove a four, placing it face down on the table.

Remove another four and place it on top of the first. Which card do you remove next? Add three to the previous number, giving you seven. Remove a seven and place it down, and then another seven.

Add three, giving you ten. Remove *one ten* and place it face down on the other cards. Add three, giving you 13. King is the equivalent of 13, so remove a king, placing it on the pile, and then another king.

You say, "I guess we could speed this up a little." Since the king will be considered the highest card in this sequence, adding three gives you three. Pull a three from the deck and then another. Place them *together* face down on the pile. Do the same with pairs of sixes, nines, queens, twos, and fives. While doing so, murmur words to this effect: "I have to find good pairs for you to choose from." When finished, set the deck down to your left.

From top to bottom, your pile should be: 5-5-2-2-Q-Q-9-9-6-6-3-3-K-K-10-7-7-4-4. Although there are 19 cards, you've created the impression that you've selected a number of pairs.

Pick up the pile and hold it in dealing position in your left hand. Push off two cards with your left thumb and take them in your right hand, saying, "Dolores, one of these pairs is very special. Let's see which one you choose. Just tell me when." Pause and then place the pair face down on the table. Take the next pair, pause, and place them on top of the others on the table. Continue until Dolores tells you to stop. Deliberately place the pair in your hand face down in the middle of the table.

For the trick to work, you must deal *seven* pairs from the packet in your hand. So as you deal each pair to the table, count to yourself. Suppose Dolores chooses the fourth pair. Place this pair in the middle of the table. You have three more pairs to deal. Say, "You could have chosen any pair at all." Deal a pair onto the pile on the table, exactly as you did before, saying, "This one . . ." Deal another pair. ". . . or this one . . ." Deal another pair. "Or this one." Drop the remaining cards on top of the pile, saying, "Or any of the others." Pick up the pile and drop it on top of the rest of the deck.

"So here are the other pairs you could have chosen." Deal *eight* pairs face down onto the table, forming a rough circle around the pair chosen by Dolores. If you place succeeding pairs next to each other, observant spectators may notice that adjacent pairs have a card in common. So make sure the pairs are well separated.

"Let's see what these other pairs are." Turn over each pair, showing that each consists of unmatched cards. Ask Dolores to turn over her pair. She has selected the only matched pair.

Note

If the spectator hasn't chosen a pair by the time you've lifted off the eighth pair, drop these back on top, pick up the cards on the table and place them on top. Say, "Let's try again." Or, with a wry smile: "Perhaps you didn't understand; you're supposed to pick a pair."

Do As I Do

This is the name given to a popular type of card trick involving two decks of cards. This is probably the easiest and one of the most deceptive.

Ask Bernie to shuffle both decks of cards and then give one to you. You need to catch a glimpse of the bottom card of your deck; here's an amusing way.

Say, "This is called a 'do-as-I-do' experiment. First, you do as I do, and then I do as you do. Thus, we establish a mutuality which may work a miracle."

Tap the top of your deck three times. Wait for him to do the same with his deck. If he doesn't, say, "Please, do as I do." Lift your cards to about a 45° angle lengthwise and even them by tapping them on the table (Illus. 30). As you do so, glimpse the bottom card and remember it. (If I'm fortunate enough to get a glimpse while he is shuffling, I eliminate this step, but I still use the basic patter.)

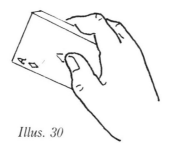

Illus. 30

Pick up your deck in your left hand and clear your throat. Chances are he will pick up the pile but not clear his throat. "Did you hear me?" Clear your throat again. After he clears his throat, say, "Now it's your turn to lead, and I must follow." (Sometimes a spectator will start to repeat what you say. "No, no," you insist, "it's your turn to lead.") Continue: "Slowly deal your cards into a face-down pile and stop whenever you want to. I'll do exactly the same."

When you both stop dealing, say, "Now it's my turn to lead again. I'll peek at the last card you dealt and remember it." Peek at the last card he dealt, but disregard it. He peeks at the last card you dealt. "Hold that card in your mind."

Place the cards in your hand on top of your pile on the table. Bernie does the same. Reach over and give his deck a complete cut. He reaches over and gives yours a complete cut.

Pick up your deck and begin fanning through, faces towards you, saying, "Find the card you're thinking of, and I'll do the same." When you come to the card you glimpsed, remove the card next to it (the one nearer the face of the deck), and place it face down on the table. Bernie places his card face down on the table. Have him turn them both over. They are the same.

Murder Most Foul

In this trick, Brother John Hamman created a unique method of forcing a card; my simplified adaptation involves no sleight of hand.

Fan the deck with the faces towards you and cut the queen of hearts to the bottom (the position nearest you). "Time for a murder mystery," you explain, "and I'll need all the face cards." Fan through the deck, jogging all the face cards up about 1½″ to 2″, except for the queen of hearts, which will remain on the bottom of the deck. Strip the other face cards from the deck and place them face down on the table. Set the deck face down to one side.

"The murder takes place in the living room of this old mansion," you say, indicating the stack of face cards. "I have to make sure all of the cast is in position." Fan through the cards, faces towards you, setting the cards up in this order from back to front: queen of diamonds, black queen/king of diamonds, black king/jack of diamonds, black jack/king of hearts, black king/jack of hearts, black jack/black queen.

The setup is quite easy to remember. Study Illus. 31 and you'll see that I've divided the cards into pairs—a red card followed by a black card in each pair. So all you need do is remember the red cards: From the top down, QD, KD, JD, KH, JH. Then have a black card of the same value follow each red card. And remember that the bottom card must be a

Illus. 31

black queen. As you set up the cards, you might chat along these lines: "In any murder mystery, there are two critical questions: Who will be the victim, and then later, who was the murderer? We start off knowing neither. But we do know that both the murderer and the victim must be one of these people. First, the victim."

Close up the cards and hold them face down in the dealing position. Fan off the top two cards, keeping them in the same order, and show them to the group. "The victim could be one of these ladies." Place the cards on the bottom. Show the next two. "Or one of these older gentlemen." Place them on the bottom. "Or one of these younger men." Show two jacks and place them on the bottom. "Or one of these older gentlemen." Show another pair of kings and place them on the bottom. "Or one of these younger men." Show another pair of jacks and place them on the bottom. "Or one of these ladies." Show the two queens and *drop them on top.*

No one will notice that you show the queen of diamonds twice.

"The lights go out, and there is a wild scramble," you announce. Rapidly perform the following: Fan out the three top cards and transfer them to the bottom, then two, then one, then three, and finally two. In all, you transfer 11 cards. Go for speed; the sloppier, the better. In effect, you have performed a false shuffle, keeping the stack intact.

"A shot rings out." Snap the cards. Hand them to a spectator. "The lights go on again. We'll let you decide who the victim is. Deal off some cards one at a time into a face-down pile and stop when you think you've found the victim."

You must now force a red card on Beth. Every second card is red, so you know that the queen of diamonds is second, the king of diamonds is fourth, the jack of diamonds is sixth, the king of hearts is eighth, and the jack of hearts is tenth. Suppose Beth deals off five cards. Tell her to look at the card on top of the packet in her hand, and to show it around. Avert your head while she does so. You know that the card is the jack of diamonds.

Suppose she deals off eight cards. Tell her to look at the last card she dealt, which you know is the king of hearts.

Tell her to replace the card in the packet and to shuffle the cards. "You know the victim, but now you must discover the murderer."

Here's Brother Hamman's subtle force.

You know what card represents the victim, so you'll now force the choice of the queen of hearts as murderer. If the victim is a king or jack, say, "We should probably choose a member of the opposite sex to be the victim. If the victim was a woman, we should make the murderer a man."

If it is the queen, say that the victim should probably be a member of the same sex. "If the victim was a man, we should make the murderer a man."

Now for the suit. If the suit was diamonds, say, "We should probably make the suit the same color, but a different suit. If the victim was in the spade suit, the murderer should be a club."

If the suit was hearts, say that the choice should be of the same suit as the victim.

"So who is the murderer?" The answer is the queen of hearts. "You're the detective, Beth. You'll have to find her. Deal the cards face up one at a time."

No murderer! "Where can she be?" you ask. "I'll bet she's hiding in the basement." Show your hands empty, then take the deck in one hand and turn it face up. There she is!

Shifting Faces

My version requires no sleights.

"I need nine face cards," you say as you fan through the cards, faces towards you. Cut a king to the top. As far as the audience knows, you've just cut a face card to the bottom. Fan through and find another king. Separate the cards at that point and slip the king to the bottom. All of this is done quite openly.

In the same way, slip a queen to the bottom, and then a jack. Continue on until you have the following eight cards on the bottom, the last one being the bottom card: K Q J J K Q Q J. (The suits are irrelevant.) Think of the order as two sequences of K Q J. In the first sequence, you double the jack; in the second, you double the queen.

Take the bottom eight cards off the deck, faces towards you. Casually show the bottom card of the deck. Set the deck face down on the table. Turn your packet face down. You've already said that you need nine face cards, so there's no need to mention the number.

Fan out the top three cards, take them off the packet, and show them to a spectator. "King, queen, jack. Right?" Right. Place the three on the bottom of the packet. In the same way, show the next three to another spectator, repeating your comment. Also place these on the bottom. Repeat the procedure with a third spectator. Actually, one of the cards you showed the first spectator is in the group shown to the third spectator. (Incidentally, you can show the trick to just one person. I've never had anyone note that a card in the third group has already been shown.)

Drop the packet on top of the deck. Time for a pause. Say, "So we have three groups, with a king, queen, and jack in each group. Even I can figure that out." Fan out the top three cards, take them off the deck, and place them on the table. Say, "Three." Fan off three more and place them on the others, saying, "Three more." Do it once more, saying, "And three more."

Pick up the packet and take off the top card, a jack, and drop it face up on the table. Point to it, saying, "This is the card that makes it all work." Pick up the jack and slap it against the packet several times, saying whatever magical words occur to you. Place the jack, still face up, on the bottom of the packet.

One by one, deal the top three cards (the kings) face up, overlapping them. Next to them deal the next three cards (the queens) face up. And next to the queens, deal the jacks face up. The last jack, of course, is already face up.

A Calculating Trick

While toying with the deck, sneak a look at the top card.

"A deck of cards can serve many purposes," you expound. "I like to use mine as a calculator. Let me show you."

Place the deck on the table and ask a volunteer to cut off a pile of cards and place it on the table.

"Turn over the card you cut to," you say, pointing at the card.

Suppose a four is turned over, and the card you peeked at is a nine. Make a statement along this line: "Four people are at a party. Five more arrive. How many do you have?"

"Nine," says your helper.

Turn over the nine. "That's how my calculator works."

You might repeat the stunt exactly. I prefer, before I start, to peek at the top card *and* the bottom card. That way, I can do another demonstration immediately.

You've already used the nine on top of the deck, and you know that the bottom card is a seven. Replace the deck in its original order, saying, "Let's try it again in a slightly different version."

Indicate that the spectator is to cut the deck again. "Turn your pile over," you say, indicating the pile that was cut off.

Let's say the bottom card of the pile is a six. You might say, "Six. I have six silver dollars, and I win one dollar at roulette. How many dollars do I have?"

"Seven."

Turn your pile face up, revealing the seven on the bottom.

If you have to deal with face cards, point out that a jack counts as 11, a queen as 12, and a king as 13.

Occasionally, a person will cut a card whose value matches yours. Simply propose a problem where zero is added or subtracted: "Four girls were playing jump rope in the school yard. No one joined them. How many girls were jumping at the end of recess?"

Note

If a table isn't available, perform the trick in your hands. As before, sneak a peek at the top card. Place the deck on the

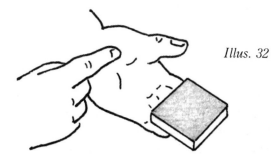

Illus. 32

outer end of your extended left fingers. Point to the inner side of your hand, indicating that this is the direction in which the spectator is to cut (Illus. 32). Proceed as with the table version.

Twin Picks

Cheryl cuts off a small pile from the top of the deck. Anthony cuts off a larger pile. Both count their cards and remember the number. The two piles are put together and shuffled.

You take the cards. Go to Cheryl, saying, "I want you to note and remember the card at your number." Take off the top card and show it to her, saying, "One." Place the card face down on the table. Show her the rest of the cards, stating each number, and placing the cards on top of one another on the table. After you show the last card, slide it under the rest, scooping up the others. It now becomes the bottom card of the group.

Go to Anthony, asking him to note the card at his number. Show him the cards in the same way as you did for Cheryl. Gather up the cards. Say, "At the count of three, I'd like you both to state the name of your card loudly and clearly. Despite the confusion, I will be able to distinguish the names of both chosen cards. One, two, three!"

They both name the same card.

"Good! I won't have to bother."

The Counter

The cards are thoroughly shuffled by a spectator. You take the deck and deal face down two cards, one on top of the other. Continue doing this until you have ten *separate* sets of two on the table. While your back is turned, as many spectators as wish pick up a set, memorize the two cards, and replace them on the table. Either you or a spectator gathers up the pairs, putting one on top of the other.

"Let's really separate those pairs," you say, dealing them into two separate piles. Place one pile on top of the other. Spectators may give the pile as many complete cuts as they wish. Now deal the cards out face up in this order:

11	1	5	8	10
15	12	2	6	9
18	16	13	3	7
20	19	17	14	4

It's an easy pattern to remember if you take it in steps:

```
1
    2
        3
            4


1   5
    2   6
        3   7
            4


1   5   8
    2   6   9
        3   7
            4


    1   5   8  10
        2   6   9
            3   7
                4
```

If you look at the original layout, you'll see that with the remaining ten cards you simply repeat the pattern, only moving to the left instead of the right.

Remove two coins from your pocket, saying, "These are coins with mystic powers. They have the power to help me locate your cards." Have a spectator place a coin next to each row in which his card appears. If both cards are in the same row, he places both next to the row.

After he does this, you can instantly identify the two cards. Wally Wilson pointed out to me that the correct way to do this is to pick up a coin which sits by a particular row, hold it up to your ear, and listen to it. Explain that the coin will whisper to you the name of the card. Nod your head, and then reveal the name. Do the same with the other coin.

Have another spectator place the coins by the rows in which his cards lie. Again let the coins whisper to you the correct names. Repeat for all others who have chosen pairs.

How do you do it? Let's start with both coins next to a single row. In Row 1, they will be cards 1 and 2. In Row 2, they will be cards 2 and 3. In Row 3, they will be cards 3 and 4. In Row 4, they will be cards 4 and 5.

There is an easy formula to apply when two *different* rows are marked by coins:

Note which of the two rows is the lower number. (Rows 2 and 4 are marked, for instance. The lower number is 2.) The *row number* tells you the position of the selected card in the other row. It will be at the corresponding number, *counting from the left*. (In our example, Row 2 is marked, so 2 is the critical number. Go to the other row and, starting at the left side, count over two cards. It's one of the selections.)

To get the other selection, subtract the number of the higher-numbered row from 5. (In the example, the higher-numbered row is 4. Subtract 4 from 5, giving you 1.) In the other row, the second chosen card will be at the corresponding number, *counting from the right*. (You go to the lower-numbered row—Row 2—and start counting from the right side. You don't get very far, however. Since the key number is 1, the other selection must be the first card on the right side of the row.)

Let's try a few more examples. A spectator places his

coins by Rows 1 and 3. 1 is the lower number, so you know
that one of the selections is the 1st card on the left in Row 3.
Subtract 3 from 5 and you get 2. In Row 1, the other selection is 2nd from the right.

Let's take another look at the layout. This time I'll show
the same number for matching pairs.

1	1	5	8	10
5	2	2	6	9
8	6	3	3	7
10	9	7	4	4

Let's try another example. Let's suppose the coins are by
Rows 1 and 2. 1 is the lower number. So one selection is the
1st card on the left in Row 2. Subtract 2 (the number of the
higher-numbered row) from 5, giving you 3. The other selection is 3rd from the right in Row 1. Consulting the above
chart, you will note that the 5s match.

The Queen's Quilt

Wally Wilson introduced this trick to me. In the original, 16
cards were laid out, folded up, and the kings were reversed
among the others. In my version, there's a lot more laying
out and rolling up.

Let's examine precisely how the quilt is folded. To follow
along, remove from the deck these cards in any suit: A, 2, 3,
4, 5, 6, 7, 8, 9. Deal them out *face up,* as shown in Illus. 33.
Turn the following face down: 2, 4, 8. The layout should
resemble Illus. 34. (This is the appropriate layout first used
in the trick.)

When folding the quilt, you may turn over rows and columns in any order you wish until you end up with one pile.
You must, however, choose an *outside* row or column each
time.

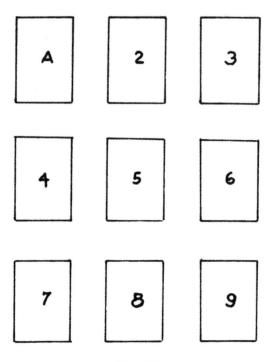

Illus. 33

Before each folding, envision the layout as an actual quilt, with the cards sewn together, as shown in Illus. 35. The "thread" is indicated by broken lines. Suppose you decide to fold over the right side of the quilt first. The column of cards on the right would be folded over, just as though they were connected (Illus. 36). Actually, of course, the cards are turned over individually. And as each card is turned over, it's placed on the appropriate adjacent card. *In effect,* however, the column is rolled over as though the cards were connected. Fold over the cards in the right column; check and make sure your layout is exactly like that shown in Illus. 36. Now return the cards to the layout shown in Illus. 34 and 35.

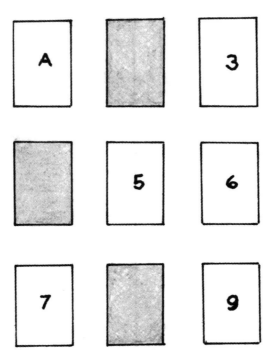

Illus. 34

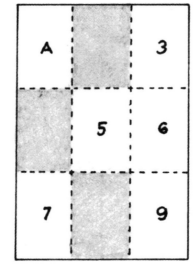

Illus. 35

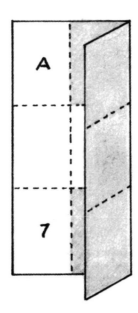

Illus. 36

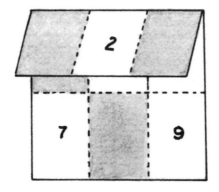

Illus. 37

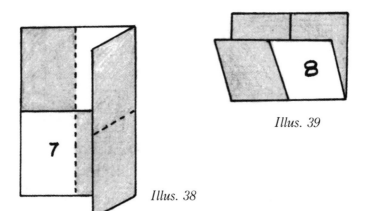

Illus. 39

Illus. 38

Instead of folding over the right column, suppose you decide to fold over the top portion of the quilt first. The top row of cards would be turned over, just as though they were connected (Illus. 37). Roll over the top row and check it against Illus. 37.

Suppose that next you wish to fold over the right side of the quilt. The right column of cards would be rolled over, just as though they were connected (Illus. 38). Again, roll over the right column and check it against the illustration.

Next you decide to fold up the bottom row. The result is shown in Illus. 39. Roll your bottom row and check it. You now have two piles side by side. You could turn over either pile and place it on top of the other. In our example you'll fold over the pile on the left.

Pick up the pile and glance through it. You'll find that one card is face down—the six. In every instance, the critical card or cards will face the opposite direction to the rest of the cards.

Now for the trick itself. You need a simple setup which can be made in advance, or which you can make openly while chatting with the spectators. From the top of the deck down, you should have three kings, a spot card, and three queens. Toss face up onto the table the other king and queen, along with the jack of spades.

Hold the deck face up in your left hand as you begin your tale. "In the olden days, a rogue named Jack the Juggler came to court." Indicate the jack of spades. "You might know him as the jack of spades. He was granted an audience by the king and queen." Indicate the king and queen on the table. As you proceed with the story, place the king and queen on the bottom of the deck. (The order of the two doesn't matter.) Then stick the jack of spades in so that it's the fourth card from the bottom. "Jack the Juggler told the king, 'Sire, I would give you a magic quilt. If you are pleased, I would hope for the reward of a small purse full of gold.' The king agreed. Jack reached into his big bag and took out a quilt made of nine sections."

You're holding the deck face up in your left hand. Take nine cards from the face of the deck, taking them *one under the other.* Set the rest of the deck aside *face down.* Turn the nine-card packet face down. Deal the nine cards face down in this order, as you look at them:

```
1   2   3
4   5   6
7   8   9
```

"Jack then marked a big K on the magic quilt," you continue. The cards at the following positions should now be turned face up: 8, 4, 2. The *face-down* cards are circled:

```
①   2   ③
4   ⑤   ⑥
⑦   8   ⑨
```

From the spectators' view the remaining face-down cards form a rough K. Point this out.

"The K," said Jack, "stands for King. And when we fold the quilt and say the magic words, we'll have inside a beautiful portrait of the king. And *that's* what's magic about the quilt."

A spectator, with your help, is now to fold up the quilt. He is to start at any one of the *outside* rows or columns. Don't provide a long-winded explanation; instead, as he makes his choices of a row or column, demonstrate, guide, and assist him.

After the spectator has folded the nine cards into a single pile, pick up the pile, saying, "Jack picked up the folded quilt and said these magic words, 'Without an oath or any cursin' / Give us a portrait of my favorite person.' " Fan out the cards so that the faces are towards yourself. Spectators will see the reversed jack of spades. "But there was only a portrait there of Jack the Juggler." Toss the jack out face up on the table. "The king wanted to behead him, but Jack pleaded for another chance. Reluctantly the king agreed."

While saying this, note the position of the king among the

cards facing you. Cut the cards so that the king will be the top card on the face-down packet. Turn the packet face down and stick the jack of spades into the middle somewhere.

"So Jack got out another quilt." Deal the cards out exactly as before. "But the king said, 'I want a bigger quilt.' Jack said, 'No problem, Your Majesty.' " You now move the two cards on your near left towards you, so that the layout looks like this:

$$1 \quad 2 \quad 3$$
$$4 \quad 5 \quad 6$$
$$7 \quad 8 \quad 9$$

From the top of the deck, deal three cards (the kings) into the open spots. (These cards will be designated by numbers 10, 11, 12.) Set the deck aside again. The layout now looks like this:

$$1 \quad\ \ 2 \quad\ \ 3$$
$$4 \quad\ \ 5 \quad\ \ 6$$
$$10 \quad 11 \quad 9$$
$$7 \quad\ \ 8 \quad 12$$

While moving the cards and adding the kings, say, "Jack said, 'Nothing to it. We just cut a few patches, move a few patches, add a few patches, and do a little sewing.' "

Once the layout is set up, continue, "Jack said, 'Since I'm the magician, we probably should have used *my* initial.' So he put a big J on the quilt."

Turn over cards at positions 3, 5, 11, 9, 8, and 12. The *face-down* cards are circled in this layout:

$$①\quad ②\quad 3$$
$$④\quad 5\quad ⑥$$
$$⑩\quad 11\quad 9$$
$$⑦\quad 8\quad 12$$

Call the spectators' attention to the J fashioned by the face-down cards.

As before, have a spectator repeat the business of folding up the quilt. Pick up the pile and, like Jack, say the magic words, "If you can do anything / Give me a portrait of the king."

Fan the cards so that the reversed kings face the spectators. Say, "When they spread out the quilt, there were four beautiful pictures of the king." Take the kings from the packet and toss them out face up. Note the position of the queen in the cards facing you. Cut the cards so that the queen becomes the *bottom card* of the face-down packet. Turn the packet face down. Gather up the kings and place them on the bottom.

"The king said, 'I'll give the quilt to my queen, for she'll love these beautiful pictures of me. And I'll give you a purse full of gold. But I'll need a *big* quilt for myself. So, for another purse of gold, make me another quilt.' Jack said, 'No problem, Your Royal Highness.' Jack got out another blanket and laid it out." Lay out the 12 cards face down like this:

$$1 \quad 2 \quad 3 \quad 4$$
$$5 \quad 6 \quad 7 \quad 8$$
$$9 \quad 10 \quad 11 \quad 12$$

" 'That blanket isn't any bigger,' said the king, 'it's only wider.'

" 'Your Majesty isn't as dumb as he looks,' said Jack. 'No problem, sire.' " As you now move the cards about and add the queens, say, as before, " 'We just cut a few patches, move a few patches, add a few patches, do a little sewing—and *voilà!*' "

First, move the cards at positions 1 and 2 closer to the spectators. Then move the cards at positions 5 and 6 to the positions formerly occupied by 1 and 2. The layout:

```
1   2
5   6   3   4
        7   8
9  10  11  12
```

Deal the top four cards (a spot card, followed by three queens) into the open spaces. From the top down, these are designated as 13, 14, 15, 16.

```
1    2   15   16
5    6    3    4
14   13   7    8
9   10   11   12
```

The position of these four cards is critical. The queens must lie at these positions if the trick is to work:

```
X   X   Q   Q
X   X   X   X
Q   X   X   Q
X   X   X   X
```

"The king said, 'And we must use the royal K, instead of that silly J.' Jack said, 'Of course we must.' So Jack made a K on the quilt." Turn the cards at these positions face up: 2, 15, 5, 3, 14, 13, 9, 11. *Face-down* cards are circled:

```
①    2   15   ⑯
5    ⑥    3    ④
14   13   ⑦    ⑧
9   ⑩   11   ⑫
```

Point out that the face-down cards resemble a K.

Once more a spectator folds the blanket. Pick up the pile and say the magic words for Jack: " 'Now a portrait, at my command, / Of the ruler of this land."

Sure enough, when you spread out the cards, you have four lovely portraits of the ruler of the land—the queen.

Notes

Don't attempt this trick until you can perform every single movement automatically. This means plenty of practice. Once you have all the moves down perfectly, work on your patter, developing funny lines of your own.

Here's an amusing way to end the trick. Before performing, place a jack of spades from an old deck into your pocket so that it's facing outward. Make sure you *borrow* a deck to do the trick.

After the first folding, in which the portrait of Jack the Juggler appears, say, "The king said, 'Off with his head!' So Jack ran and hid behind the drapes." Place the jack of spades face outward *behind* the jack of spades in your pocket. Show the queen and say, "The queen begged the king to show a little mercy, so he relented." Place the remaining eight cards on the bottom of the deck. " 'Come on out,' the king said, 'and try another quilt.' " Hand a spectator the deck face up and ask him to deal off nine cards. As he does this, remove the old jack of spades from your pocket and, without showing its back, set it aside face up on the table. Make sure the king is the top card of the packet.

Take the nine-card packet and lay it out. Take the deck and, from the top, add the three kings as directed above. Proceed to the end of the trick, first showing all kings, and finally all queens.

"Again the king said, 'Off with his head!' And *this* time he meant it." Pick up the jack of spades resting on the table and tear off the top third, making sure no one sees the back. Toss the pieces face up on the table.

Act very pleased with yourself, thanking all for their attention. The owner of the deck will probably display some chagrin. You might tell him, "I can see you're upset. It so happens that I brought an extra jack of spades with me. You can have it." Give him the jack of spades from your pocket.

Incidentally, with the cards from an old deck, you can do

this ending 52 times. Suppose you've placed the eight of clubs in your pocket. At the beginning of the trick, take the eight of clubs from the spectator's deck, saying, "There once was a travelling magician, symbolized by the eight of clubs . . ."

Quadruple Coincidence

Preparation: On top of the deck you should have the ace, king, queen, jack, and ten of spades—a royal flush. They may be in any order, but the ten should be the third card down.

Start by riffle-shuffling the deck, keeping your stack on top. Now give the deck *one* overhand shuffle. Just pick up the bottom three quarters of the deck and shuffle these cards onto the top section. Your stack will be intact somewhere in the deck. Invite the spectators to give the deck a few complete cuts.

Say, "I'd like to demonstrate a simple fact: You can't beat the odds. If I place one card here on the table and someone chooses four cards at random, one of those cards will almost certainly match my choice. It's a matter of probability. So let's test it out."

Ask Steve to assist you. Tell him, "I'll choose a card—my prediction card. And I'll give you four chances to match it in value. I'm sure you can do it. In fact, I'd bet money on it, except that I'd be taking advantage of you."

Fan through the cards, faces towards yourself. Find the ten of spades. Cut the cards so that this becomes the top card, saying, "This is a perfect prediction card." Without letting anyone see it, take it from the deck and set it face down on the table.

The position: The ten of spades is face down on the table;

two cards of the royal flush are on top of the deck and two on the bottom.

Set the deck face down on the table and ask Steve to cut off a substantial portion. Take the cut-off cards from him and set them aside. Point to the bottom portion, saying, "Please deal those into two piles, alternating." When he finishes, the top card of each pile will be a card from the royal flush.

Point to the pile you set aside. "Cut off some of those, please." He cuts off a pile. Take the remainder and place them face down on top of your prediction card, saying, "We won't need these anymore, so we'll let them guard my prediction card."

Have Steve deal the cards he cut off into two more piles, alternating. When he finishes, the *bottom* card of each of these two piles will be a card from the royal flush.

"Let's give you even more choices," you say. Have him place the first two piles he dealt on top of the second two piles he dealt.

At this point, the top and bottom card of each of the two piles is a card from the royal flush. Have him pick up either pile. "Deal those into a pile and stop whenever you wish." When he stops, have him place the remaining cards on the table.

Have him pick up the other pile. He deals these into a pile, stopping when he wishes.

"Perfect! I'm sure that at least *one* of your choices will match my prediction card."

Turn over the pile which has your prediction card on the bottom, setting it on the table face up. "The ten of spades. Now let's see if we have a match."

Turn over one of the other piles so that it's face up on the table. Register disappointment, then say, "That's all right; I have three more chances."

Turn over another pile and react the same way. By this time, spectators are increasingly aware of what's happening.

Turn over another pile and demonstrate considerable irritation. After you turn over the last pile, say sardonically, "Great! Not a single match!" Continue chatting as everyone else, of course, notices the royal flush. Make sure you leave enough time for all to notice it. Say, "I swear this works 99 percent of the time. I don't know what went wrong." Shrug and shake your head, displaying total dejection as you gather up the cards.

Note
Clearly, if you prefer, you may have *two* spectators do the cutting and dealing, providing a bit more audience involvement.

MASTERY LEVELS CHART & INDEX

Lie like a Rug	78	*		
Lonely Pair	98			*
Lots of Luck	40			*
Lucky Card Location	11		*	
Most Magicians	68		*	
Murder Most Foul	102			*
Mystic Prediction	81		*	
Nine to One	45	*		
Number, Please	42			*
One & Only	56	*		
Over & Over	50			*
Perfectly Mental	80	*		
Phony Coincidence	58	*		
Poker Location	18		*	
Prediction Plus	87		*	
Prints of Magic	12	*		
Quadruple Coincidence	122		*	
Queen's Quilt	111			*
Shifting Faces	105		*	
Simple Speller	41	*		
Something to Sniff At	60	*		
Stop Sign	55		*	
10-Card Trick	22			*

Twin Picks	108	*		
Weight for Me	92			*
What's on Your Mind?	91		*	
What's Up?	52		*	
You Might Wonder	75	*		